Field Guide to
Personality Disorders
Second Edition

A Companion to Disordered Personalities

David J. Robinson, MD
Fellow, American Psychiatric Association
Fellow, Royal College of Physicians and Surgeons of Canada

Rapid Psychler® Press

Suite 374
3560 Pine Grove Ave.
Port Huron, Michigan
USA 48060

Suite 203
1673 Richmond St.
London, Ontario
Canada N6G 2N3

Toll Free Phone   888-PSY-CHLE (888-779-2453)
Toll Free Fax   888-PSY-CHLR (888-779-2457)
Outside the U.S. & Canada — Phone 519-667-2335
Outside the U.S. & Canada — Fax 519-675-0610
website   www.psychler.com
email   rapid@psychler.com

ISBN 1-894328-10-8
Printed in the United States of America
© 2005, Rapid Psychler® Press
Second Edition, First Printing

Dedication

To my aunt
Arlene Dickinson

and my cousin
Keith Franzen

Rapid Psychler® Press 🚲
produces books and presentation media that
are:
- Comprehensively researched
- Well organized
- Formatted for ease of use
- Reasonably priced
- Clinically oriented, and
- Include humor that enhances education, and
  that neither demeans patients nor the
  efforts of those who treat them

Acknowledgments

I am indebted to the following individuals for their unfailing support and enthusiasm in assisting me with this text.

- **Monty & Lilly Robinson**
- **Brian & Brenda Chapman**
- **Dr. Donna Robinson & Dr. Robert Bauer**
- **Brad Groshok & Susan McFarland**
- **Tom Kay and Randy Keron**

Many of the nurses, medical students, psychiatry residents, occupational therapists, social workers, secretaries, and consultant psychiatrists at the London Health Sciences Center, South Street Campus in London, Canada gave me helpful suggestions over the years that have been incorporated into this book. Thanks everyone!

I am indebted to **Martha Wilke** for her diligent research in putting together the material on the psychological tests and assessments that appear in Chapter 6.

I would like to acknowledge several of my former supervisors whose clinical acumen inspired my interest in personality disorders: **John Mount, MD; John Wiener, MD; Rima Styra, MD; Nikkie Cordy MEd; Allan Tennen; Paul Steinberg, MD**

Editorial Bored

I am very fortunate to have a group of friends and colleagues who read the early drafts of this book and made numerous suggestions regarding both style and content. Their input was invaluable and I am indebted to them for their kind assistance. This is a much better book because of your efforts. A special thank you to:

- **Sandra Northcott, MD (Editor Emeritus)**
- **Sue Fletcher-Keron, RCS**
- **Martha Wilke, BScOT**
- **Maria Santos, MA**
- **Rob Zalan, MD**
- **Vinay Lodha, MD**
- **Riyadh Bin Daham, MD**
- **Noel Laporte, MD**
- **Marnie Desjardins, RN**
- **Tom Norry, BScN**
- **Heidi Haensel, MD**
- **Hae-Ryun Park, MD**
- **Lyudmila Burdan, MD**

Table of Contents

Dedication. iii
Acknowledgments. iv
Changes to the Second Edition xi
Publication Notes. xii

Chapter 1
Introduction & Diagnostic Principles. 1

1.1   Why Study People with Personality Disorders?. 2
1.2   What is a Personality?. 4
1.3   What is a Personality Disorder?. 5
1.4   How Do I Diagnose a Personality Disorder?. 8
1.5   General Diagnostic Criteria for a
       Personality Disorder. 10
1.6   Diagnostic Infobits. 11
1.7   A Brief Critique of DSM Axis II Constructs. 12
1.8   What is the ICD-10?. 13
1.9   Symptom Versatility. 14
1.10   An Integrated Classification System. 15
1.11   Confused About Clusters?. 16
1.12   Personality Change Due to a General Medical
       Condition. 17
1.13   References. 18

Chapter 2
Cultural Factors. 19

2.1   Culture and Personality. 20
2.2   Specific Cultural Examples. 21
2.3   References and Suggested Reading. 23

Chapter 3
Therapeutic Principles. 25

3.1   Introduction. 26
3.2   Models of Psychological/Personality Development. . . 27
3.3   Life Cycle Stages. 28
       Jean Piaget. 28
       Erik Erikson. 29
       John Bowlby. 30
       Margaret Mahler. 31

Sigmund Freud. 32

3.4 Attachment Theory & Object Relations Theory. 33

What is Attachment Theory?. 33

What is Object Relations Theory?. 34

3.5 Basic Psychodynamic Principles. 37

Transference. 37

Countertransference. 38

Resistance. 39

3.6 What is Cognitive Therapy?. 40

Basic Concepts. 41

Basic Strategies. 41

Some Cognitive Distortions. 42

Course of Cognitive Therapy Sessions. 43

3.7 What is Group Therapy?. 43

3.8 What is Interpersonal Therapy?. 45

3.9 Integrating Therapeutic Strategies. 48

3.10 References. 49

Chapter 4
Ego Psychology & Ego Defenses. 51

4.1 What is Ego Psychology?. 52

4.2 Classification of Ego Defenses. 55

4.3 Mnemonic for Ego Defenses. 56

4.4 Ego Defenses in Personality Disorders. 57

4.5 Ego Defenses Illustrated. 58

Repression. 58

Acting Out. 59

Controlling. 60

Denial. 60

Displacement. 61

Dissociation. 61

Distortion. 62

Idealization/Devaluation. 63

Identification. 64

Inhibition. 64

Intellectualization. 65

Introjection. 65

Isolation of Affect. 66

Passive-Aggression. 66

Projection. 67

Projective Identification. 67
Rationalization. 70
Reaction Formation. 70
Regression. 71
Schizoid Fantasy. 71
Sexualization. 72
Somatization. 72
Splitting. 73
Undoing. 73
4.6   Mature Ego Defenses. 74
Anticipation. 74
Humor. 75
Sublimation. 75
4.7   References. 76

Chapter 5
Biological Dimensions. 77

5.1   What Does "Psychosomatic Mean?". 78
5.2   What is the Biopsychosocial Model?. 80
5.3   The Biopsychosocial Management Plan. 81
Investigations. 82
Short-Term Treatment. 83
Longer-Term Treatment. 84
5.4   Biology and Personality. 85
Temperament and Character. 86
5.5   Addressing Temperament in Treatment. 94
5.6   Personality Disorders as Milder Forms of Major
Psychiatric Disorders. 96
5.7   The Mental Status Examination (MSE). 99
5.8   A Rationale for the Use of Psychotropic Medication. . 100
The Dimensional Model. 100
Genetic/Temperamental Factors. 102
Co-Existing Axis I & II Disorders. 103
5.9   Selection of Medication. 104
Neuroleptics/Antipsychotics. 106
Mood Stabilizers. 106
Antidepressants. 107
Sedative-Hypnotics. 107
Others. 107
5.10   Limitations in the Use of Medication. 108

5.11 What About "Chemical Imbalances?"............. 109
5.12 Special Considerations......................... 109
    Medication as an Entity...................... 110
    Separate Providers.......................... 111
5.13 References.................................. 113

Chapter 6
Psychological Testing &
Diagnostic Interviews.................115

6.1 How Can Psychological Testing Help
    to Make a Diagnosis?......................116
6.2 Projective Assessments........................ 117
    Forer Standard Sentence Completion Test....... 117
    Holtzman Inkblot Test....................... 118
    Rorschach Ink Blots......................... 119
    Rotter Incomplete Sentences Blank............. 119
    Thematic Apperception Test.................. 120
6.3 Objective/Structured Assessments............... 121
    Borderline Personality Organization Scale....... 121
    Coolidge Assessment Battery.................. 122
    Diagnostic Interview for Borderlines, Revised..... 123
    Dimensional Assessment of Personality
        Pathology — Basic Questionnaire............. 124
    Eysenck Personality Questionnaire — Revised..... 125
    International Personality Disorder Examination... 126
    Millon Clinical Multiaxial Inventory — III........ 127
    Minnesota Multiphasic
        Personality Inventory — II................... 128
    NEO Five-Factor Inventory................... 129
    NEO Personality Inventory — Revised........... 129
    Omni-IV Personality Disorder Inventory......... 130
    Personality Assessment Inventory.............. 130
    Personality Assessment Schedule.............. 131
    Personality Diagnostic Questionnaire — IV....... 131
    Personality Disorder Interview................ 132
    Schedule of Nonadaptive and
        Adaptive Personality...................... 133
    Standardized Assessment of Personality......... 134
    Structured Clinical Interview for DSM-IV
        Personality Disorders..................... 135

      Structured Interview for DSM-IV
        Personality Disorders. 135
      Structured Interview for Five-Factor Model
        of Personality. 136
      Wisconsin Personality Disorders Inventory. 137
6.4   Diagnostic Interviews. 138
6.5   References. 138

Chapter 7
Personality Changes in Later Life. 139
7.1   Introduction. 140
7.2   DSM-IV-TR Description of Personality Disorders. . . . 140
7.3   Difficulties in Using DSM-IV-TR Diagnostic Criteria. .141
7.4   Adult Psychological Development. 142
7.5   Personality Changes in Older Age. 143
7.6   What is the Longitudinal Course of
        Personality Disorders?. 145
7.7   Treatment Planning for Elderly Patients. 146
7.8   Personality and the Process of Change. 148
7.9   Personality and the Process of Psychotherapy. 149
7.10   References. 151

Chapter 8
Other Personality Topics. 153
8.1   Multiple Personality Disorder/Dissociative
        Identity Disorder. 154
8.2   Masochistic (Self Defeating) and
        Sadistic Personalities. 158
8.3   The Organic Personality/Personality Change Due
        to a General Medical Condition. 160
8.4   The Inadequate Personality. 162
8.5   The Asthenic Personality. .163
8.6   The Cyclothymic Personality. 164
8.7   The Explosive Personality. 165
8.8   References. 166

Chapter 9
Personality Disorder Humor. 169
      The Schizoid Personality. 170

The Paranoid Personality. 171
The Schizotypal Personality. 172
The Histrionic Personality. 173
The Antisocial Personality. 174
The Borderline Personality. 175
The Narcissistic Personality. 176
The Avoidant Personality. 177
The Dependent Personality. 178
The Obsessive-Compulsive Personality. 179
Parking Lot of the Personality Disordered. 180
Bistro of the Personality Disordered. 181
Why Did the Chicken Really Cross the Road?. 182
Personalities 'R Us Corporate Structure. 183
The Mutation of Ego Defenses. 185
Nag-B-Gone. 186
If You Love Something, Set It Free. 187
Shopping by Diagnosis. 188
Newhart Was Never Like This. 189
Paranopoly. 195
Anatomy of a Romance Novel. 196
Anatomy of a Bond Adventure. 197
8-Ball Cologne. 198
Sociopathy 101. 199
Fatal Personalities Instinctively Attract. 200
InnerSpace, The Interpersonal Frontier. 201
First Date Checklist. 202
Dependent's Apartment (from date with Avoidant). . 203
Rules of Order for the Malignant Obsessive-
      Compulsive Personality. 204
Lady Macbeth Knows Dirt!. 205
The Fractionated Personality Disorder. 206

Index. **208**

About the Author and the Artist. **212**

Changes to the Second Edition

The second edition of *Field Guide* was completely re-conceptualized to be a companion for *Disordered Personalities*, which is a primer that provides an introduction to the diagnosis and management of the DSM-IV-TR personality disorders. The previous edition of *Field Guide* was strictly a condensation of *Disordered Personalities*. There is no longer any overlap of material between the new editions of these titles.

Field Guide introduces topics that are necessary to understand in conjunction with the diagnostic criteria and recommended management for personality disorders. At well over 400 pages, *Disordered Personalities* was starting to feel like a rather thorough primer, but with over 30 sections per chapter, this is the intended purpose of this title. Separating out the material contained in the *Field Guide* made sense for both practical and educational purposes.

Instead of using humor, *Disordered Personalities* uses movie examples to help provide with a quick way of familiarizing themselves with the topic. I wanted *Field Guide* to keep humor as its educational enhancer, and have made extensive use of the superb work generated by my artistic collaborator, Brian Chapman. His illustrations always capture the essence of the material being presented with a humorous spin. He has contributed many new drawings for this edition.

Lastly, there was no room in *Disordered Personalities* for the humorous articles and illustrations included in previous editions. I have received so many favorable comments on this material and was strongly encouraged to include it in one of my publications.

Thank you for supporting my work!

Dave Robinson

London, Canada   May, 2005

Publication Notes

Terminology

Throughout this book, the term "patient" is used to refer to people who are suffering and who seek help while bearing pain without complaint or anger. The terms "consumer" or "consumer-survivor" reflect an unfortunate trend that is pejorative towards mental health care, labeling it as if it were a trade or business instead of a profession. These terms are also ambiguous, as it is not clear what is being "consumed" or "survived." Where possible, I used the genderless "they" to refer to patients. When gender needed to be specified, I alternated between male and female.

Graphics

All of the illustrations in this book are original works of art commissioned by Rapid Psychler Press and are a signature feature of our publications. Rapid Psychler Press makes available an entire library of color illustrations (including those from this book) as 35mm slides, overhead transparencies, and in digital formats (for use in programs such as PowerPoint®). These images are available for viewing and can be purchased from our website — **www.psychler.com**

These images from our color library may be used for presentations. We request that you respect our copyright and do not reproduce these images in any form, for any purpose, at any time.

Bolded Terms

Throughout this book, various terms appear in **bolded text** to allow for ease of identification. Many of these terms are defined in this text. Others are only mentioned because a detailed description is beyond the scope of this book. Fuller explanations of all of the bolded terms can be found in standard reference texts.

Chapter 1

Introduction
&
Diagnostic
Principles

1.1 Why Study People with Personality Disorders?

I have had the chance to peruse many texts and articles about personality disorders, and noticed that they rarely start out by saying anything encouraging about the topic. I was similarly inclined in the previous editions of this book as well as *Disordered Personalities*, which is the companion primer on the DSM-IV-TR personality disorders. There must be something that compels authors and researchers to want to write about these disorders, and I believe that this has to be emphasized at the outset.

You are reading this book because you have an interest in people. What makes individuals so interesting is the endless diversity in their idiosyncrasies, quirks and unique qualities — in other words, their personalities. I think this is beautifully summed up in the title of a book by Isabel Briggs Myers (1995), called *Gifts Differing*. If people didn't have their eccentricities and passions, we wouldn't have anywhere near as many of the comforts in our society that we currently enjoy. One wry observer (source unknown) said that, *"nothing of significance is achieved by a reasonable person."*

Personality disorders encompass all the aspects of other psychiatric conditions that make them interesting to learn about and treat, including:
• Genetic contributions
• Psychosocial contributions
• A wide range of severity
• A wide range of treatment options
• A challenging learning curve
• Many areas of active research
• A compelling need for more effective methods of assessment and treatment

In contrast to many major clinical illnesses in psychiatry, people with personality disorders can generally be managed on an outpatient basis and usually have some supports and resources available to them. When they make even incremental changes in their lives, the benefits are obvious and often reflected in productive work or more harmonious relationships, both of which are a direct benefit to society.

The chronicity of interpersonal difficulties is often cited as a reason why clinicians shy away from treating people with personality problems. Yet, the outlook for many other psychiatric conditions is at best modest, with chronicity being the expectation. Patients with many medical diseases, such as atherosclerosis or diabetes, are treated with the expectation that their illnesses can be modified or controlled, but not cured.

One of the tenets of **dialectical behavior therapy (DBT)** put forth by Marsha Linehan (1993) is that there is that patients with personality disorders are doing the best that they can, and they need to be assisted in developing new skills to help solve their problems. It is easy to believe that patients are willfully causing difficulties for themselves and others, and if they just would "stop it," then it would make it easier for everyone. But patients with personality disorders have blind spots for their contributions to their problems, and even if they do recognize them, they do not usually have effective strategies for getting back on track. They required the help of skilled therapists and this need is a genuine as any other in psychiatry, or in other areas of medicine.

As Joel Paris (2003) points out, *"All therapists treat patients with personality disorders. Some do so by choice, others by chance."* Personality disorders are not merely ten listings in the DSM-IV-TR, they describe people with problems in fundamental areas of living. Learning leads to understanding, which in turn leads to tolerance.

1.2   What is a Personality?

The word "personality" is used in different contexts. We hear gossip about "TV personalities," learn that someone we haven't met yet has "a nice personality," and may refer to our favorite beer as "full of personality." An operational definition of the term is useful to have for work in clinical settings.

One definition of **personality** is *a relatively stable and enduring set of characteristic behavioral and emotional traits.* Over time, a person will interact with others in a reasonably predictable way. However, as the adage "don't judge a book by its cover" warns, circumstances can alter behavior, so that someone does something "out of character." For example, extreme circumstances like divorce, New Year's Eve or the Superbowl can bring out behavior that is atypical for that person.

Personality changes with experience, maturity, and external demands in a way that promotes **adaptation** to the environment. It is affected by genetic (internal), psychosocial and interpersonal (external) factors. While a discussion on the theory of personality is beyond the scope of this book, enumerating some of the etiologic factors is helpful in understanding personality disorders.

The majority of behaviors in non-humans are thought to be genetically programmed. The process of natural selection influences the survival of a species so that those having a better fit with their environment are more likely to endure. Our distant ancestors survived because of behaviors that sustained life and promoted reproduction. Predation, competition, attracting a mate or helper, banding together as a group, and avoiding overcrowding were all important adaptive strategies. One branch of our central nervous system is geared to a *flight, fright or fight* response, because these responses are essential for survival.

A degree of social judgment is inherent in deciding what determines a personality disorder. In different cultures, what is considered normal varies widely, necessitating that ideas, feelings and behaviors be understood in the context of that person's particular social milieu.

1.3   What is a Personality Disorder?

The preceding section on personality development sets the framework for understanding disorders of personalities. When genetic endowment is too loaded, early nurturing too deficient, or life experiences so severe (or interactions of these variables) that emotional development suffers, a personality disorder can often be the result.

A **personality disorder** is a variant, or an extreme set of characteristics that goes beyond the range found in most people. The American Psychiatric Association defines a personality disorder as *"An enduring pattern of inner experience and behavior that deviates markedly from the expectations of the individual's culture, is pervasive and inflexible, has an onset in adolescence or early adulthood, is stable over time, and leads to distress or impairment."*
Source: DSM-IV-TR, 1994, p. 686

While many other definitions exist, features consistently emphasized in defining a personality disorder are that it:
• Is deeply ingrained and has an inflexible nature
• Is maladaptive, especially in interpersonal contexts
• Is relatively stable over time
• Significantly impairs the ability of the person to function
• Distresses those close to the person

Personality disorders are enduring patterns of perceiving, thinking, feeling and behaving that remain consistent through the majority of social situations. An essential point is that personality disorders are **egosyntonic**, meaning that an individual's behaviors do not directly distress the person, but impact on those with whom the person interacts. An essential aspect of evaluating personality takes into account how those close to the person are affected.

The criteria with which personality disorders are diagnosed are very much within the realm of common human experiences. Each one of us at times has been: hypervigilant, destructive, suspicious, shy, bossy, vain, striving for perfection, dramatic, afraid to be alone, fearful of rejection, purposely late for something, too independent, too needy, critical of others, resentful of authority, averse to criticism, bored, seductive, or experiencing rapidly shifting emotional states. None of these behaviors alone warrants the diagnosis of a personality disorder. Instead, clusters of behaviors existing over a lengthy time period and interfering with a person's level of functioning make a diagnosis.

By basing diagnostic criteria on these common qualities and behaviors, many important questions arise:
- How many criteria are needed to make a diagnosis?
- How long do maladaptive behaviors have to be present in order to make a diagnosis?
- What degree of severity is required for feelings, perceptions, thoughts or behaviors to be considered diagnostic criteria?

Again, **adaptation** is a key point. Society has changed more rapidly than our innate adaptive strategies. A personality disorder can be considered as being an extreme behavior that, if present to a lesser degree, might be a benefit to that person. Consider patterns derived from social evolutionary strategies that are either amplified or are a poor fit for our highly individualized and technological society:

Attitude or Behavior	Personality Disorder if Taken to an Extreme
Suspiciousness, vigilance towards the environment	Paranoid
Interest in one's self — "looking out for #1"	Narcissistic
Need to be attached to others	Dependent
Meticulous attention to detail, high level of productivity	Obsessive-Compulsive
Reluctance in social situations; strong desire for solitude	Avoidant/Schizoid
Need to be able to get others' attention	Histrionic
Taking advantage of available "opportunities" or bending the rules	Antisocial
Strong desire for individuality of style and non-conformity of thought or behavior	Schizotypal

At evolutionary or social advantage of borderline personality disorder is less obvious, but this condition shares many elements of other personality disorders, particularly dependent, histrionic, antisocial, and schizotypal.

1.4   How Do I Diagnose a Personality Disorder?

In 1952, the American Psychiatric Association (APA) published the first edition of **Diagnostic and Statistical Manual of Mental Disorders (DSM)**. There were five categories with a total of twenty-seven personality disorders. Diagnoses were made using a general clinical description which was influenced by psychoanalytic concepts.

DSM-II was introduced in 1968. In this edition the number of personality disorders was reduced to twelve, though many from DSM-I were shifted to other categories of clinical disorders. Again, diagnoses were presented as descriptive paragraphs. Because of this, DSM-II was deemed by many to lack validity and inter-clinician reliability. Introduced at a time of sweeping cultural and social change, its shortcomings necessitated significant changes for the next edition.

Introduced in 1980, **DSM-III** listed specific diagnostic criteria for its fourteen personality disorders. These were first established from the psychiatric research done by Feighner, Robbins & Guze and later expanded by Spitzer. Five major changes were introduced:
- Descriptive features were based on presenting symptoms that were atheoretical and not based on presumed etiologic factors
- Information beyond the criteria was included, such as demographic, etiologic and prognostic variables
- Discrete criteria were used (e.g. symptoms, duration, etc.)
- In response to criticism about the potential misuse of labeling patients with a psychiatric diagnosis, the APA stressed using clinical judgment when applying the checklist of diagnostic criteria
- The concept of a multi-axial diagnosis was introduced, which fostered a multifaceted approach towards understanding patients

Adapted from Turkat, 1990

DSM-III-R (R for revised) was introduced in 1987. Despite the many advances in DSM-III, many clinicians felt that there were problems with the validity, accuracy and clarity of some of the criteria. The personality disorders were now also grouped into clusters based on their phenomenologic overlap:

Personality Disorder Clusters

Cluster A: Odd or Eccentric, ("Mad") — Paranoid, Schizoid, and Schizotypal.

Cluster B: Dramatic, Emotional or Erratic, ("Bad") — Antisocial, Borderline, Histrionic, and Narcissistic.

Cluster C: Anxious or Fearful, ("Sad") — Avoidant, Dependent, and Obsessive-Compulsive, (Passive-Aggressive/Negativistic was previously placed in this cluster).
See also p. 16

DSM-III-R contained eleven personality disorders; three from DSM-III were amalgamated into a new category called *Personality Disorder Not Otherwise Specified (NOS)*, which was used for conditions where it was clear a personality disorder existed, but the criteria for a specified condition were not met.

In 1994, **DSM-IV** was released, retaining the multi-axial diagnostic approach and personality clusters listed above. The number of personality disorders was reduced to ten. The **passive-aggressive personality disorder (PAPD)** was deemed to be in need of further study and was moved to Appendix B as a condition requiring further study. It was also given the alternate name of **negativistic personality disorder (NegPD)**.

DSM-IV-TR (TR for Text Revision) was released in 2000. It did not alter any of the personality disorder criteria from DSM-IV, but made minor modifications to the text accompanying the description of the disorder. The introductory text was updated, and the *Associated Features and Disorders* Section for the following conditions was revised:
- Antisocial personality disorder
- Borderline personality disorder
- Dependent personality disorder
- Obsessive-compulsive personality disorder

PAPD/NegPD appears in Appendix B with the same proposed criteria as in DSM-IV.

1.5 General Diagnostic Criteria for a Personality Disorder

A. An enduring pattern of inner experience and behavior that deviates markedly from the expectations of the individual's culture. This pattern is manifested in two (or more) of the following areas:
(1) cognition (i.e., ways of perceiving and interpreting self, other people, and events)
(2) affectivity (i.e., the range, intensity, lability, and appropriateness of emotional response)
(3) interpersonal functioning
(4) impulse control

B. The enduring pattern is inflexible and pervasive across a broad range of personal and social situations.

C. The enduring pattern leads to clinically significant distress or impairment in social, occupational, or other important areas of functioning.

D. The pattern is stable and of long duration and its onset can be traced back at least to adolescence or early adulthood.

E. The enduring pattern is not better accounted for as a manifestation or consequence of another mental disorder.

F. The enduring pattern is not due to the direct physiological effects of a substance (e.g. a drug of abuse, a medication) or a general medical condition (e.g. head trauma).

Reprinted with permission from DSM-IV-TR
© American Psychiatric Association, 2000

1.6   Diagnostic Infobits

DSM-IV-TR uses five **axes** to make a complete diagnostic summary:
- **Axis I:** Major Psychiatric Syndromes or Clinical Disorders
- **Axis II:** Personality Disorders and Mental Retardation
- **Axis III:** General Medical Conditions
- **Axis IV:** Psychosocial and Environmental Problems
- **Axis V:** Global Assessment of Functioning (GAF) Score from 0 to 100)

The DSM also uses Axis II to record prominent **personality traits** and **defense mechanisms.** For example, if a patient meets most but not all of the criteria for a paranoid personality disorder, this is recorded as "paranoid personality features." If a personality disorder or strong features are not evident but the patient uses a defense mechanism to a maladaptive level, this is recorded as "frequent use of projection." Other official entries for coding on Axis II can be "no diagnosis" or "diagnosis deferred."

The paranoid, schizoid, schizotypal and antisocial personality disorders are not diagnosed if they are coincident with certain Axis I conditions. Exclusion criteria are not given for the other personality disorders. The antisocial personality disorder is the only diagnosis with an age requirement and a prerequisite diagnosis. Patients must be at least age eighteen, and have met the criteria for a diagnosis of **conduct disorder** before the age of fifteen.

The personality disorders are not diagnosed exclusive of one another, allowing concurrent diagnoses to be made. In practice, there is usually one disorder that is more prominent and this is recorded as the Axis II diagnosis with the others listed as "features." If two or more are equally apparent, they are all recorded.

The residual personality diagnosis in the DSM-IV-TR is called **personality disorder not otherwise specified (NOS).** This is used when the patient does not meet the complete criteria for a single personality disorder, but exhibits specific diagnostic features of other personality disorders. Additionally, if the criteria are met for the depressive or passive-aggressive/negativistic personality disorders, the diagnosis of personality disorder NOS is used.

The diagnostic criteria for personality disorders in the DSM-IV-TR are listed in decreasing order of significance (where this is established).

DSM-IV-TR also lists severity and course specifiers for diagnoses:
- Mild: Few, if any, symptoms in excess of those required to make the diagnosis are present, and symptoms result in no more than minor impairment in social or occupational functioning
- Moderate: Symptoms/functional impairment between mild and severe
- Severe: Many symptoms in excess of those required to make the diagnosis, or several symptoms that are particularly severe, are present, or the symptoms result in marked impairment in social or occupational functioning

1.7 A Brief Critique of DSM-IV-TR Axis II Constructs

The DSM has been widely criticized both for its specific content and its general aim to be a "catalog" or "shopping list" of mental disorders. While some detractors certainly have valid points, it has given psychiatry a basis for diagnostic uniformity and an accurate means for describing psychopathology. The specialty was in virtual disarray without DSM because diagnoses were made subjectively and there was no standard for terminology.

The DSM continues to improve with each edition. Each of the criteria for every diagnosis is reviewed by committees of highly-respected researchers and clinicians who overhaul the entire concept and make evidence-based alterations from edition to edition (much to the dismay of those of us who must wade through and memorize the changes).

Each personality disorder has a minimum of seven key diagnostic criteria, which ranges up to nine for some conditions. DSM-IV-TR doesn't enumerate all of the possible criteria for these disorders, it includes those that are valid in differentiating adaptive from nonadaptive feelings, thoughts and behaviors. Similarly, all of the ways that someone's personality can go awry cannot be coalesced into only ten different conditions. Again, the personality disorders listed have survived the scrutiny of decades of reliability and validity studies and are well enough established to merit inclusion. Rather than applying a "label," it is crucial to be able to accurately diagnose psychiatric conditions. A diagnosis is a key first step in helping patients. After establishing a diagnosis, a management plan develops involving investigations and treatment for biological, social and psychological factors.

Medical records are legally required to contain a diagnosis which is used for a variety of statistical purposes. These results then make an impact on funding, research and clinical initiatives.

1.8   What is the ICD-10?

The DSM-IV-TR isn't the only diagnostic system available. The ICD-10 is the **International Classification of Diseases, Tenth Edition**, published by the **World Health Organization (WHO)** in 1992. It is the diagnostic classification system used outside North America (mainly in Europe). Preparation of DSM-IV-TR was coordinated with Chapter V of the ICD-10, called *Mental and Behavioural Disorders*.

DSM-IV-TR coding and terminology are compatible with the ICD-10, which is eventually planned to be introduced in the United States. The DSM-V will have even greater integration with the ICD. The ICD-10 has in common with DSM-IV-TR the following personality disorders: paranoid, schizoid, histrionic, and dependent.

Some slight changes in name between the two systems are as follows:
• The antisocial personality is called dissocial/dyssocial
• The obsessive-compulsive is called anankastic/anancastic
• The avoidant personality is called anxious

There is a diagnostic category called the emotionally unstable personality disorder with a borderline type and an impulsive type. The latter has no clear DSM-IV-TR analogue.

Narcissistic personality disorder in DSM-IV-TR has no equivalent in the ICD-10 (which may account for some cultural differences).

Schizotypal personality disorder is considered to be a major clinical disorder in the ICD-10 and is called schizotypal disorder.

1.9   Symptom Versatility

A maxim in psychiatry is that no single symptom is exclusive to a particular diagnosis. The personality disorders, particularly those in the same cluster, share an overlap of symptoms:

Avoidant Personality Disorder (APD)
↓ ↑
social isolation; avoids interpersonal contact
↓ ↑
Schizoid Personality Disorder (SzdPD)
↓ ↑
expression of emotion (affect) is constricted; few friends outside family
↓ ↑
Schizotypal Personality Disorder (SztPD)
↓ ↑
suspiciousness or paranoid ideation
↓ ↑
Paranoid Personality Disorder (PPD)
↓ ↑
self-referential grandiosity (all events pertain to the person)
↓ ↑
Narcissistic Personality Disorder (NPD)
↓ ↑
interpersonally exploitative; lacks empathy
↓ ↑
Antisocial Personality Disorder (ASPD)
↓ ↑
impulsivity; failure to plan ahead; shallow expression of emotion
↓ ↑
Histrionic Personality Disorder (HPD)
↓ ↑
rapidly shifting moods; affective instability
↓ ↑
Borderline Personality Disorder (BPD)
↓ ↑
unable to tolerate being alone or with feelings of abandonment
↓ ↑
Dependent Personality Disorder (DPD)
↓ ↑
reluctant to delegate tasks; trouble with project completion
↓ ↑
Obsessive-Compulsive Personality Disorder (OCPD)
↓ ↑
restricted involvment in pleasurable activities; often anxious
↓ ↑
Avoidant Personality Disorder (APD)

1.10 An Integrated Classification System

Clusters A, B & C were described above and are based on descriptive or phenomenological similarities. The integration of etiologic, therapeutic, prognostic and conceptual variables provides a method of classification based on **spectrum, self** and **trait** features.

Spectrum Disorders share a biological link to major disorders with a spectrum of expression; these tend to have poorer prognoses. Schizotypal and paranoid personalities are considered to be within the schizophrenia spectrum of disorders.

Self Disorders cause severe dysfunction; they are often linked to turbulent personal backgrounds, a fragile sense of identity and an unstable course. Personality disorders in this category include schizoid personality disorder (schizophrenia spectrum) and antisocial and borderline personality disorders (mood disorder spectrum).

Trait Disorders exist on a dimension with normality; sufferers may be subjectively distressed in social, occupational, and cultural contexts. The prognosis for these conditions is widely considered to be more favorable. The trait disorders are listed below along with a simple scheme for classifying them on two factors: independence/dependence and introversion/extroversion.

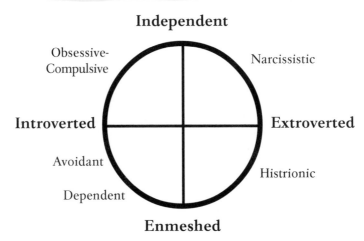

1.11   Confused About Clusters?

Cluster A Personality Disorders have an overlap with psychotic disorders and are considered to be in the schizophrenia spectrum of illnesses. The genetic and/or environmental factors that cause more serious conditions such as schizophrenia or schizoaffective disorder are thought be operative, but to a lesser degree. Cluster A personality disorders have also been classified as cognitive disorders (Paris, 2003).

Cluster B Personality Disorders share an overlap with mood and impulse-control disorders. They are also considered to be disorders with externalizing symptoms.

Cluster C Personality Disorders have an overlap with anxiety disorders and are considered to be disorders with internalizing symptoms.

1.12 Personality Change Due to a General Medical Condition

Changes in personality can be caused by medical conditions, the effects of medications, or drugs of abuse. It is imperative to investigate the possibility that a personality change is due to medical factors because any psychiatric disorder can be mimicked by somatic causes. The personality change must be persistent, and a clear change from the person's previous patterns. When this happens, the DSM-IV-TR refers to it as **personality change due to a general medical condition.** Proper diagnostic classification is to place *Personality Change Due to . . . (Condition)* on Axis I and the specific medical condition on Axis III, e.g.

Axis I: Personality Change Due to Hypothyroidism
Axis III: Hypothyroidism

Diagnostic Criteria

A. A persistent personality disturbance that represents a change from the individual's previous characteristic personality pattern.
(In children, the disturbance involves a marked deviation from normal development or a significant change in the child's usual behavior patterns lasting at least 1 year.)
B. There is evidence from the history, physical examination, or laboratory findings that the disturbance is the direct physiological consequence of a general medical condition.
C. The disturbance is not better accounted for by another mental disorder (including Mental Disorders Due to a General Medical Condition).
D. The disturbance does not occur exclusively during the course of a delirium and does not meet criteria for a dementia.
E. The disturbance causes clinically significant distress or impairment in social, occupational, or other important areas of functioning.

Specify Type

Labile, Disinhibited, Aggressive, Apathetic, Paranoid, Other, Combined, Unspecified

1.13 References

American Psychiatric Association
Diagnostic and Statistical Manual of Mental Disorders, 4th Edition, Text Revision
American Psychiatric Association, Arlington, VA, 2000

American Psychiatric Association
Diagnostic and Statistical Manual of Mental Disorders, 4th Edition
American Psychiatric Association, Washington, DC, 1994

American Psychiatric Association
Diagnostic and Statistical Manual of Mental Disorders, 3rd Edition, Revised
American Psychiatric Association, Washington, DC, 1987

American Psychiatric Association
Diagnostic and Statistical Manual of Mental Disorders, 3rd Edition
American Psychiatric Association, Washington, DC, 1980

American Psychiatric Association
Diagnostic and Statistical Manual of Mental Disorders, 2nd Edition,
American Psychiatric Association, Washington, DC, 1968

American Psychiatric Association
Diagnostic and Statistical Manual of Mental Disorders
American Psychiatric Association, Washington, DC, 1952

Briggs Myers I
Gifts Differing: Understanding Personality Type
Davies-Black Publishing, Mountain View, CA, 1995

Linehan MM
Cognitive Behavioral Treatment of Borderline Personality Disorder
The Guilford Press, New York, 1993

Paris J
Personality Disorders Over Time
American Psychiatric Publishing, Inc., Arlington, VA, 2003

Sperry L
Handbook of Diagnosis & Treatment of the DSM-IV Personality Disorders
Brunner/Mazel, New York, 1995

Turkat I
The Personality Disorders
Pergamon Press, Elmsford, New York, 1990

World Health Organization
Pocket Guide to the ICD-10 Classification of Mental & Behavioural Disorders
American Psychiatric Press Inc., London, England, 1994

Chapter 2

Cultural Considerations

2.1   Culture and Personality

While the DSM-IV-TR is prepared and published by the American Psychiatric Association, it is used by clinicians for ethnically diverse populations within the United States as well as in other countries. A number of features in DSM-IV-TR specifically address cultural aspects:

• A section outlining cultural factors (where applicable) in the description of the disorder which accompanies the diagnostic criteria; this is generally included with age and gender-specific considerations

• An outline for cultural formulation which assists clinicians in evaluating and more accurately being able to assess the impact of the illness within the individual's cultural context (this appears in Appendix I on p. 897)

• A glossary of culture-bound syndromes (also in Appendix I)

Personality disorder criteria in particular can be difficult to apply across cultural situations. Concepts of self, coping mechanisms and modes of emotional expression vary considerably between cultures. The World Health Organization has emphasized the similarity in psychiatric illnesses between cultures and that diagnostic constructs are applicable regardless of culture. The increasing amount of information about genetic contributions to psychiatric disorders supports this view. Paris (1991) reported on the WHO multi-site investigation of personality disorder diagnoses on four continents. The findings suggest that the majority of personality diagnoses made would be applicable in all centers.

Epidemiologic studies have consistently shown the prevalence of Axis II conditions across populations to be in the range of 1 - 3% for each diagnosis. Accordingly, cultural factors have not been consistently shown to have a dominant role in the etiology of personality disorders.

As noted above, DSM-IV-TR and the ICD-10 do not have a complete overlap in their cataloging of personality disorders, indicating that cultural factors affect the determination of an "ideal personality." Foulks (1996) states that the major issue for clinicians having to make diagnoses across cultures is differentiating between the ideal personality type, the typical personality type and the atypical personality from the standpoint of cultural functionality. Culture, a pervasive environmental factor, does influence which traits are adaptable in a certain milieu. While some of these styles may not ultimately be desirable, they assist functionality. Individuals may have done well with their personality characteristics in their own culture, but encountered difficulties upon relocating to a society that does not value the expression or suppression of certain behaviors to the same degree.

2.2   Specific Cultural Examples

• Reyes & Lapuz (1963) found the predominant personality style to be histrionic (then called hysterical) in Pilipino culture. Paranoid personality features were also frequently reported, because there are widespread beliefs that supernatural forces control one's destiny.

Maloney (1976) reports that in Mediterranean cultures, there is belief in the "evil eye" as well as other paranoid personality features: perceiving personal and threatening messages in neutral events, expecting to be harmed by others without reason to warrant this concern, and a widespread reluctance to share personal information with others in case it might be used against the person.

Canino & Canino (1993) describe indigenous healing practices among Puerto Rican peoples involving witchcraft, magic, herbs and potions. While these beliefs have an overlap with the Schizotypal Personality Disorder, it is a widespread cultural belief that it is the job of each person to perfect his or her spirit, with progress being made by successfully dealing with life's trials. Indigenous healers are known as *espiritistas* and *espiriteros*, and are often more frequently sought for assistance than are workers in traditional mental health clinics (Garrison, 1971).

Kinzie & Leung (1993) and Kim (1993) report on some of the difficulties in treating patients from Southeast Asia. In particular, poor compliance with medications, concern about "saving face" by discussing only positive factors in therapy and being late or missing appointments entirely are described. While these behaviors have may appear to be narcissistic in nature, there are culturally based in that development of trust with therapists is not as automatic as in Western cultures and reflect an ambivalence towards forms of treatment that are a considerable variance with their traditional approaches.

• Fujii, Fukushima & Yamamoto (1993) provide a description of several cultural features in treating Japanese patients:
—Delaying visits to mental health professionals in order to avoid shame and humiliation (avoidant personality characteristics)

—Excessive devotion to work, studying, and competitive pursuits (obsessive-compulsive personality characteristics)

—Belief in a form of passive love called *amae*, which is "to depend and presume upon another's benevolence" and describes a dependency-need relationship (dependent personality characteristics)

References and Suggested Reading

Alarcón RD, Foulks EF & Vakkur M
Personality Disorders and Culture: Clinical and Conceptual Interactions
Wiley & Sons, New York, 1998

American Psychiatric Association
Diagnostic and Statistical Manual of Mental Disorders, 4ᵗʰ Edition, Text Revision
American Psychiatric Association, Washington DC, 2000

Canino IA & Canino GJ, in
Culture, Ethnicity & Mental Illness
Gaw AC, Editor
American Psychiatric Press Inc., Washington, DC, 1993

Foulks EF, in
Culture & Psychiatric Diagnosis: A DSM-IV Perspective
Mezzich JE, Kleinman A, Fabrega H & Parron DL, Editors
American Psychiatric Press, Inc., Washington, DC, 1996

Fujii JS, Fukushima SN & Yamamoto J, in
Culture, Ethnicity & Mental Illness
Gaw AC, Editor
American Psychiatric Press Inc., Washington, DC, 1993

Garrison V
Supporting structures in a disorganized Puerto Rican migrant community.
70ᵗʰ Annual Meeting of the American Anthropological Association
New York, December, 1971

Gaw AC
Concise Guide to Cross-Cultural Psychiatry
American Psychiatric Press, Inc., Washington DC, 2001

Group for the Advancement of Psychiatry (GAP Report 145)
Cultural Assessment in Clinical Psychiatry
American Psychiatric Press, Inc., Washington DC, 2002

Kinzie JD & Leung PK, in
Culture, Ethnicity & Mental Illness
Gaw AC, Editor
American Psychiatric Press Inc., Washington, DC, 1993

Kim LIC, in
Culture, Ethnicity & Mental Illness
Gaw AC, Editor
American Psychiatric Press Inc., Washington, DC, 1993

Maloney J
The Evil Eye
Columbia University Press, New York, 1976

Mezzich JE, Kleinman A, Fabrega H, & Parron DL, Editors
Culture and Psychiatric Diagnosis: A DSM-IV Perspective
American Psychiatric Press, Inc., Washington DC, 1995

Millon T with Davis RD
Disorders of Personality: DSM-IV and Beyond
Wiley & Sons, Inc., New York, 1996

Okpaku SO, Editor
Clinical Methods in Transcultural Psychiatry
American Psychiatric Press, Inc., Washington DC, 1998

Paris J
Personality disorders, parasuicide & culture.
Transcultural Psychiatric Research Review 28: p. 25-39, 1991

Reyes B & Lapuz L
The practice of psychiatry in the Philippines.
J. of the Philippines Coll. of Physicians 1(3): p. 161-165, 1963

Tseng WS & Streltzer J
Cultural Competence in Clinical Psychiatry
American Psychiatric Publishing, Inc., Arlington, VA, 2004

Tyrer P & Stein G, Editors
Personality Disorders Reviewed
Gaskell/The Royal College of Psychiatrists, London, England, 1993

World Health Organization
Pocket Guide to the ICD-10 Classification of Mental & Behavioural Disorders
American Psychiatric Press Inc., London, England, 1994

Chapter 3

Therapeutic Principles

3.1   Introduction

This chapter provides a introduction to the theoretical principles and concepts contained in the individual personality chapters that follow. The first section provides a brief introduction to personality development. This is a diverse field which encompasses many theories and active areas of research that are beyond the scope of this book.

Following this, sections on ego psychology and ego defenses are presented to give an appreciation of where and how personality disorders are thought to develop. Defense mechanisms are crucial to understanding the interpersonal behavior exhibited by those with personality disorders. Defenses that are discussed in the later chapters are introduced here by means of a definition and illustration. These concepts can prove to be a challenge when learning about personality disorders, so the extra dimension of a caricature has been added.

Following the ego defenses, the next section introduces the major psychodynamic principles. These key concepts form the building blocks of many types of psychotherapy and are relevant to all interactions with patients. **Attachment theory** and **object relations theory** are also outlined to help understand psychodynamic aspects.

Next, the basic tenets of cognitive, group and interpersonal psychotherapy are presented. **Psychotherapy,** which is the major form of treatment   personality disorders, can be defined as:
Treatment by communication for any form of treatment for mental illnesses, behavioral maladaptations, and/or other problems that are of an emotional nature, in which a trained person deliberately establishes a professional relationship with a patient for the purpose of:
• *Removing, modifying, or reducing existing symptoms*
• *Attenuating or reversing disturbed patterns of behavior*
• *Promoting positive personality growth and development*
Source: Campbell, 2004

Inherent in this definition is the application of a set of theoretical principles to the person's difficulties. This provides the roadmap the therapist will use to guide the therapy.

The following chapter presents the biological dimension, including an introduction to the genetic aspects of character (e.g. temperament) and the rationale for using medications (psychopharmacology) in the treatment of personality disorders.

Recent advances in neuro- and biological psychiatry have renewed interest in genetic and neonatal factors. Bio-genetic factors that can provide a more descriptive classification system are continually sought. This approach is fueled by the growing understanding of the genetics of major psychiatric conditions and that some of the personality disorders may be attenuated forms of these conditions.

Innate characteristics or tendencies can be reinforced or extinguished by relationships early in life. Whatever the genetic contributions, social and psychological influences have an impact from the moment of birth. Early disruptive experiences with caregivers are strong influences for later personality disorders, though curiously not everyone exposed to potentially "pathogenic" situations develops a disorder. Genetic endowment and experience dynamically interact to shape personality. Overall, genetic endowment sets a range of possibilities and, within that range, developmental experiences influence the outcome.

Many different theories exist on what goes awry in personality development. Still, an unifying, all-encompassing explanation remains elusive. Some people, despite the best-intentioned parents and a nurturing environment, still develop severe personality disorders. Others, despite disadvantage and abuse, emerge as well-adjusted people making meaningful contributions to society. This chapter presents the basics for the most common approaches to understanding and treating personality disorders.

3.2 Models of Psychological/ Personality Development

The ancient Greeks considered personality to be a mix of four temperaments with imbalances causing the following symptoms:
- Yellow bile — choleric — causing irritability and anxiety
- Black bile — melancholic — causing depression
- Mucus — phlegmatic — causing apathy
- Blood — sanguine — resulting in optimism or hypomania

It's unfortunate that things had to get more complicated than this. However, treatment needed to improve — bleeding was the remedy for excessive optimism and purgatives were given for melancholy.

Personality development is theoretically based — the variables are often too complex to establish an exact science. Many classification systems offer explanations for various stages of the personality development. Among the most famous are those of: **Jean Piaget, Erik Erikson, John Bowlby, Margaret Mahler** and **Sigmund Freud.**

3.3   Life Cycle Stages

The life cycle represents stages from birth to death. There are three assumptions about the progress through these stages.
1. Stages are completed in their given sequence.
2. Development proceeds only when an earlier stage is completed.
3. Each stage has a dominant feature, and various personality difficulties can be caused by arrested development at this stage, also know as **fixation.**

Jean Piaget

Birth to 2 years: Sensorimotor Phase
Schemata (patterns of behavior) dictate actions; the environment is mastered through assimilation (taking in new experiences through one's own knowledge system) and accommodation (adjusting one's system of knowledge to the demands of the environment); object permanence is achieved by two years.

2 to 7 years: Preoperational Phase
Feature: Uses symbolic functions; egocentrism; animism; magical thinking .

7 to 11 years: Concrete Operations
Feature: Logical thinking emerges; able to see things from another's point of view; laws of conservation are understood.

11 years to Adolescence: Formal (Abstract) Phase
Feature: Hypothetico-deductive reasoning used; able to understand philosophical nature of ideas; more flexible thinking becomes possible.

Erik Erikson

Birth to 1 year: Basic Trust versus Basic Mistrust
Feature: Consistency of caregiver is crucial.

1 to 3 years: Autonomy versus Shame & Doubt
Feature: Learns to walk, feed self and talk; firmness of caregivers, boundaries and guidelines are necessary before autonomy.

3 to 5 years: Initiative versus Guilt
Feature: Mimics adult world; **oedipal** struggles occur at this age, with resolution via social identification.

6 to 11 years: Industry versus Inferiority
Feature: Busy with building, creating, accomplishing; abilities in relation to peers increase in importance.

11 years to Adolescence: Identity versus Role Diffusion
Feature: Preoccupied with hero worship and appearance; group identity develops.

21 to 40 years: Intimacy versus Isolation
Feature: Finding love and work are the key tasks.

40 to 65 years: Generativity versus Stagnation
Feature: Guiding children/new generation avoids stagnation.

Over 65 years: Integrity versus Despair
Feature: Satisfaction with productivity and accomplishments.

John Bowlby

Birth to 12 weeks: Phase I

- Olfactory and auditory stimuli used to discriminate between people.
- Initiates innate attachment behavior to any person — smiling, babbling, reaching and grasping, which increase the time spent close to a caregiver.
- Tracks movement with eyes; stops crying in the presence of a person.

12 weeks to 6 months: Phase II

Feature: increased intensity towards the primary attachment figure.

6 months into Second Year: Phase III

Feature: Attachment to mother more solid, uses her as a base from which to explore; **stranger anxiety** towards others.

2 years and beyond: Phase IV

Feature: Growing independence from mother; obtains sense of objects being persistent in time and space; observation of adult behavior.

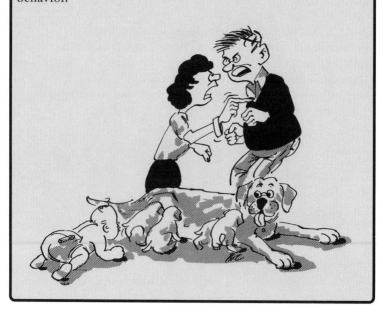

Margaret Mahler

Birth to 4 weeks: Normal Autistic Phase
Feature: Main task is to achieve equilibrium with the environment.

4 weeks to 4 months: Normal Symbiotic Phase
Feature: Social smile.

4 to 10 months: Separation Individuation — Phase I, Differentiation
Feature: **Stranger anxiety** (development of recognition memory).

10 to 16 months: Separation Individuation — Phase II, Practicing
Feature: **Separation anxiety**

16 to 24 months: Separation Individuation — Phase III, Rapprochement
Feature: The child wants to be soothed by mother, but may be unable to accept her help.

24 to 36 months: Separation Individuation — Phase IV, Consolidation and Object Constancy.
Feature: Able to cope with mother's absence; finds substitutes for her.

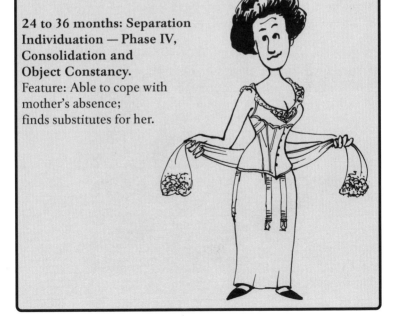

Sigmund Freud

Birth to 1 year: Oral Stage
- Main site of tension and gratification is the mouth, lips and tongue.
- More aggressive with the presence of teeth after six months.

1 to 3 years: Anal Stage
- Acquires voluntary sphincter control; anus and perineal area become the major area of interest.

3 years to 5 years: Phallic-Oedipal Stage
- Genital stimulation of interest; masturbation is common.
- Intense preoccupation with castration anxiety.
- In Freud's theory, penis envy is seen in girls at this stage.
- **Oedipus Complex** (desire to have sex with and marry opposite-sex parent and dispose of or destroy same-sex parent).

5 to 11 years: Latency Stage
- **Superego** forms, the last part of the psychic apparatus.
- The **id** is present at birth and the **ego** develops as the child becomes aware of the external world.
- Sexual drives channeled into socially acceptable avenues.
- Quiescence of sexual drive as the oedipal complex is resolved.

11 to 13 years: Genital Stage
- Final psychosexual stage.
- Biologically capable of orgasm and able to experience true intimacy.

3.4 Attachment Theory & Object Relations Theory

Ego psychology proposes that sexual and aggressive drives are innate, or primary, and relationships with people are secondary. The most important task according to this line of thought is to discharge the tension generated by these drives. **Attachment theory** and **object relations theory** propose that human drives are geared towards seeking relationships instead of discharging primal urges. In these theories, tension emerges in the context of frustrated relationships.

What is Attachment Theory?

The central concept in attachment theory is that close, positive attachments are a fundamental human need. This theory posits that the quality of early attachments to caregivers largely determines the success of future relationships. Deprivation of early attachments, with the loss, or threatened loss, of positive attachments to caregivers creates a vulnerability resulting in adverse psychological reactions. The outcome of these reactions can be a diverse array of emotional conditions, including personality disorders.

If the innate need for close attachment is satisfied by **pleasurable interpersonal relationships (PIRs)**, normal growth and development occur. If these needs are frustrated by **disturbances in interpersonal relationships (DIRs)**, an inevitable drop in self-esteem is generally followed by one of three responses:

Withdrawing, or the **flight response**, involves:
• Building interpersonal walls to diminish emotional pain
• Developing work habits that compensate for other deficiencies, or finding a structured "institutional" workplace as a substitute
• Regressing to the need for earlier pleasures that don't require other people (these are often "oral" habits like smoking or drinking alcohol)

The **fight response** is one of aggression. Anger is a source of energy that, if not used constructively, may be used against the self, causing the emergence of suicidal feelings. Anger and hostility directed at others bring about a potent sense of guilt. Accompanying this sense of guilt is its unconscious analog — the fear of, or need for, punishment.

The third response is a **creative effort**, which involves learning how to deal with DIRs in more adaptive ways.

What is Object Relations Theory?

The word object in this theory is an unfortunate substitute for person. Freud focused his attention on the subject who possessed the drives. Object, in this context, referred to the person at whom the drive was aimed. Object relations developed from the contributions of a number of theorists, each with his or her own perspective. Some of the integral names associated with object relations are: **Melanie Klein, W.R.D. Fairbairn, Margaret Mahler, Otto Kernberg** and **Heinz Kohut.** Freud laid some of the groundwork for the development of this theory, and in many ways Object Relations is a refinement and reshaping of his ideas. There is no unified object relations theory. Each of the contributors listed above had a particular focus, though there is a common thread of agreement. Central to an understanding of object relations is that *interpersonal contact* becomes *internalized* as a *representation* of that relationship. For example, in a developing child, it is not the mother who is internalized, but the whole relationship. This process is called **introjection**. In object relations, an understanding of people and what motivates them stems from an awareness of how relationships are internalized and transformed into a sense of self or self-image in that person.

"Object" Relations?

Object relations theory postulates that the most important relationship is with an early caregiver, most often the mother. The sense of alternating gratification and deprivation occupies so much of the life of an infant that this relationship becomes a template for subsequent relationships. Consider the following interactions in a hungry infant:

One Hungry Baby: Two Possible Outcomes

Positive experience of mother: Attentive caregiver	**Negative experience of mother:** Neglectful caregiver
Positive emotional experience: Satiated with milk	**Negative emotional experience:** Persistent hunger
Positive sense of self: Loved and cared for	**Negative sense of self:** Frustrated and angry

---

These two sets of interactions are **introjected** as the **good object** and **bad object**, partitioning or **splitting** the inner world of a child into good and bad experiences. It is important to note that what is introjected is the *experience* of the relationship, not necessarily the actual relationship. For example, a loving mother attending to other responsibilities might still be experienced as the bad object. Over time, this influences the sense of self, or one's sense of being. The notion of conflict in object relations is viewed as the clash between the internalized representations of feelings, self and objects.

From this point on, the various contributors focused on different applications of this theory — defense mechanisms (especially splitting and projective identification), individual disorders (narcissistic and borderline in particular) and parameters affecting development.

An individual may find a substitute in order to compensate for deficient attachments. As a means of understanding substitution as symptom, Steinberg (1995) has divided activities into three groups:

Direct Oral or Genital Somatic Satisfaction
* Overindulgence in sex, food or alcohol/drug abuse

Narcissistic Satisfactions
* Acquisition of fame/notoriety, money or power

Investment in "Institutions"
* Excessive devotion to work, social causes, groups, or recreational activities; close attachments to animals, plants or inanimate objects

Deficient attachment early in life influences one's style of relating as an adult. Early relationships are internalized as a negative self-image and negative view of others. This has a very strong influence on how we relate to others and to whom we relate. These early relationships tend to get repeated (a process called **repetition compulsion**).

The internalized image influences what is expected in future relationships and how others are perceived. Internalized objects are projected onto others. With a personality disorder comes an inability to realistically evaluate others. This is most obvious when individuals expect someone to behave a certain way when very little is known about that person. This process is called **transference** and is explained in the next section.

Object Relations Infobits
* Object relations considers the very substance of the human psyche to be made of concerns about relationships, not discharging drives.

* The focus in Freud's theory was on the father. By causing castration anxiety in boys and penis envy in girls, the father determines the success of the **oedipal complex** or **oedipal stage**. In object relations, the focus is pre-oedipal and centers on the relationship with the mother. This places critical developmental issues in the first year of life instead of at the fifth or sixth year when oedipal issues are thought to emerge.

3.5   Basic Psychodynamic Principles

There are some time-honored principles that form the basis of psychodynamic theory and give it a unique perspective on diagnosing and treating personality disorders. As introduced earlier, the presence of the **unconscious** is an integral part of this theoretical perspective. Dreams and Freudian Slips (**parapraxes**) are the two most common ways the unconscious is accessed. Symptoms and behaviors are visible extensions of unconscious processes that defend against repressed wishes and feelings. Experiences in childhood are considered crucial in the formation of the adult personality. It is in these early years that the repetitive interactions with family members are of etiologic significance in personality disorders. Early patterns of relating to others persist into adult life; in a sense, the past is repeating itself. This was aptly put by William Wordsworth as *"the child is the father of the man."*

Transference

In therapy, the process of transference involves a patient experiencing the therapist as a significant person from his or her (the patient's) past. Feelings, thoughts and wishes that are **projected** onto the therapist stem from a previous significant relationship. In this way, the current therapeutic relationship is a repetition of the past. Properly handled, transference is fertile ground for learning in psychotherapy. Two key points characterize transference:

* The relationship is *re-enacted* in therapy, not just *remembered*; this becomes more obvious when one focuses on the **process** of the sessions with patients instead of only on the **content**
* The reaction to the therapist is inappropriate and anachronistic

Transference in not limited to therapy. It can be said that all relationships are a combination of the real relationship and transference reactions. Early attachments and internal representations of caregivers are so firmly held that they color future interactions. In this way, transference guides the relationships that people pursue. The unconscious influences behavior to a larger extent than is often appreciated. We seek out the type of relationship(s) with which we are already familiar, which is the principle of **psychic determinism**. However, there is room for choice and conscious intention in bringing about change, which is one of the goals in psychotherapy.

Countertransference

Harry Stack Sullivan said "we are all much more human than otherwise." Just as patients exhibit transference in their relationships with therapists, the converse also happens. Therapists are (usually) human beings who will, to some degree, unconsciously experience the patient as someone from their past. While many definitions of **countertransference** exist, Kernberg (1965) summed it up as *the therapist's total, conscious emotional reaction to the patient.* Whereas patients' transference is grounds for observation and interpretation, countertransference is not openly discussed in therapy. Constant internal scrutiny is required on the therapists' part to be aware of countertransference reactions. Though it can be tempting to act on such feelings, doing so only repeats the kind of relationship patients have experienced, rather than having the chance to learn about them. Instead, countertransference can be used diagnostically and therapeutically. It gives a firsthand awareness of how patients interact with others. Links (1996) lists countertransference reactions as a key step in recognizing personality disorders:

• Is a symptom disorder present?
• Why is the patient seeking help?
• How does the patient make me feel?

Use countertransference — how do
you feel about the patient?

Resistance

At some point in treatment, almost every patient exhibits a tendency to oppose therapeutic efforts. Change is often accompanied by distress because there is internal preserve to keep the psychic status quo. Whereas ego defenses are unconscious and inferred, resistance can be conscious, preconscious or unconscious and is openly observed. It can take many forms: lateness or absence from sessions, prolonged silence, digression to irrelevant material, personal questions about the therapist, "forgetting" the content of past sessions, avoidance or failure to arrange payment, non-compliance with treatment recommendations, etc.

Resistance is a self-protective mechanism against experiencing strong emotions. As therapy progresses, these "unacceptable" feelings become less repressed and some type of resistance will accompany their expression. Just as countertransference is used therapeutically, resistance also provides important information. A psychodynamic approach provides an opportunity to discover what the resistance is concealing. Though the term resistance implies that it is an impediment, understanding resistance is a large component of psychotherapeutic treatment.

By understanding the processes of transference, countertransference and resistance, the therapeutic relationship can be used to increase the awareness of how past relationships (object relations) affect current relationships, thus encouraging conscious decisions about changing maladaptive patterns of interpersonal behavior.

3.6 What is Cognitive Therapy?

A **cognition** is a verbal or visual representation that comes into consciousness when one is confronted with a situation. Specifically, it is what one thinks *in* the situation and not *about* the situation. This type of therapy was developed by Aaron Beck and is based on his observation that *"an individual's affect and behavior are largely determined by the way in which he or she structures the world."* Beck originally developed this approach for use in depressive disorders. He found that the style of thinking depressed patients exhibited reinforced a negative view of themselves, the world and their future (**the cognitive triad of depression**). Cognitive techniques are now available for many conditions, including personality disorders. Cognitive therapy is short-term, structured and interactive. It has a "here and now" focus and is geared to solving current problems. The assumptions on which cognitive therapy is based are as follows:

Cognitions represent a synthesis of internal and external stimuli
↓
Individuals structure situations based on their cognitions
↓
Emotional and behavioral changes are caused by cognitions
↓
Cognitive therapy elicits an awareness of "cognitive distortions"
↓
Correction of these distortions leads to improved functioning

Adjusting the
"cogs" in
cogntive therapy

Basic Concepts

The genesis of a personality disorder, and some Axis I disorders, is biased information processing, called a **schema**. In essence, those with personality disorders think differently than those who aren't affected. The way that information is synthesized forms the type of disorder manifested (e.g. anxious people interpret the world as threatening, depressed people visualize hopelessness, etc.). Both genetic and environmental contributions predispose patients to interpret experiences in an altered way, which can initiate the disorder.

Basic Strategies

The process of cognitive therapy involves an agreement between patient and therapist to explore and modify dysfunctional beliefs, called **collaborative empiricism.**

The next step involves the elucidation of certain themes that run through patient's misperceptions. Like psychodynamic therapies, connections are made to previous experiences, so the development of the disorder can be understood. This is called **guided discovery.**

Patients keep a diary of their **negative thoughts** or **automatic assumptions.** This becomes the focus of the therapy session. These conclusions are constantly evaluated, subjected to scrutiny and reality testing and then refined. The initial goal of cognitive therapy is to have these automatic assumptions become more neutral or benign so that emotional and behavioral reactions are lessened.

Socratic questioning guides the patient and therapist to understand the problem and examine the consequences of maintaining maladaptive thoughts and behaviors. When patients see the illogical or false aspects of their beliefs, they are encouraged to alter them in a more accurate, adaptive and reasoned way. A **cognitive shift** occurs when patients gain a more realistic and reasoned approach to processing information. This is facilitated by the exploration of maladaptive assumptions, testing their validity (reality testing) and altering them when alternative explanations or contradictory evidence is presented.

At the beginning of each session, the therapist sets the agenda, checks and assigns homework and introduces new skills. Behavioral techniques are practical interventions designed to change maladaptive strategies, such as: scheduling activities, graded task assignments, rehearsal, self-reliance training, role playing and diversion techniques.

Some Cognitive Distortions

- **Arbitrary inference:** drawing a specific conclusion without supporting evidence, or in the face of contradictory evidence.
- **Assuming Temporal Causality:** seeing an artificial or spurious connection between events that were related only coincidentally.
- **Catastrophizing:** using a small setback as evidence of gross failure.
- **Dichotomous Thinking:** seeing experiences as being all good or all bad; a complete success or an utter failure.
- **Magnification/Minimization:** seeing something as being much more or much less significant than it is in reality.

- **Overgeneralization:** developing a "rule" after a small or isolated number of incidents and applying it broadly and to unrelated situations.
- **Personalization/Excessive Responsibility/Self-Reference:** attributing external events to one's self without evidence supporting the connection.
- **Selective abstraction:** seeing a situation in terms of a single detail and ignoring other possibilities.

Course of Cognitive Therapy Sessions

Early
- Initiate relationship
- Elicit information
- Define problem, generate list, and discuss expectations
- Explain the type of therapy
- Assign homework — recognize the connection between feelings and behavior
  (e.g. count certain thoughts, record automatic thoughts)

Mid
- Focus on patterns of thinking
- Make connections between thoughts, emotions and behavior
- Challenge thoughts that interfere with functioning; progress towards altering the underlying assumptions
- The patient takes a more active approach to homework

Later
- Time-limited; 10 - 25 sessions, can go on for several months
- Date of termination is discussed in the first session
- With the intstillation of a new approach to thinking about difficulties, patients "learn to become their own therapist"

3.7   What is Group Therapy?

Group therapy is an effective form of treatment for many disorders. Virtually any type of individual therapy is possible in a group setting: supportive, cognitive-behavioral, interpersonal, analytically-oriented or educational. Groups can be set up on an inpatient or outpatient basis, be open or closed to new members, be time-limited or open-ended, and have heterogeneous or homogeneous compositions.

Group therapy is an efficient treatment modality. In an age where resources for therapy are under greater scrutiny, groups are gaining popularity and, in some cases, are an economic necessity.

While some personality-disordered patients do well in a group setting, others do not. It is important to keep in mind that within a given diagnosis, there is a range of functioning that should be considered when determining suitability for group therapy.

Group therapy is different from the *Bob Newhart Show* or the movie, *Color of Night*. A group has an identified leader or therapist who uses strategic interventions and the interactions between members to facilitate change. Unlike individual therapy, a group provides opportunities for immediate feedback from peers. Also, the group functions as a micro-society and is perhaps a more "normal" setting in which to view patients' interactions. This is valuable, because it allows the therapist and the patient to observe transference reactions to a wider variety of people.

Groups conducted for personality disorders are generally ongoing and open to new members. Ideally, a group has eight to ten members. Sessions are ninety minutes to two hours, once or twice per week. Socialization outside the group is discouraged, as is participation in concurrent therapy elsewhere. The theoretical basis for treating personality disorders in groups is usually analytically oriented. There are several powerful therapeutic factors operative in group therapy settings:

- Cohesion
- Altruism
- Universality
- Acceptance
- Socialization
- Catharsis
- Validation by other group members
- Corrective emotional/familial experiences
- Learning from group members
- Internalization
- Instillation of hope
- Existential factors
- Identification with, or imitation of, another member

Interventions in group therapy are the same as in individual psychodynamic psychotherapy, though they can be initiated by members as well as the therapist(s):

- **Confrontation** — calling attention to a trait that the person was previously unable to see; confrontations do not address motivation, they are made to point out the behavior; the group situation is particularly effective at bringing about a change in those confronted.

- **Clarification** — group members become adept at noticing repeating patterns in sessions; clarification brings in to focus particular actions

- **Interpretation** — interpretations are designed to make unconscious processes conscious and reveal the underlying motivations or conflicts; they are made to attach a significance to events, feelings and behaviors motivations and conflicts are revealed.

Group psychotherapy provides an opportunity for interpretations to be made on a group-as-a-whole and an individual basis.

Peer interpretations can be particularly valuable, as members frequently have less difficulty learning about themselves with input from other group members. However, peer interpretations have a higher chance of being incorrect, poorly timed, or somehow skewed. In general, groups function more smoothly when members direct their attention to confrontation and clarification, leaving the more delicate matter of interpretation to the group leader.

3.8   What is Interpersonal Therapy?

Interpersonal therapy (IPT) focuses on the interactions between the patient and significant others. In IPT, is it assumed that personality disorders result as a function of disordered relationships. The central aim in therapy is to elucidate and alter the inadequate, inappropriate and self-defeating means of communicating with current family members, the family of origin, present romantic partners and friends.

As with other theories, there is no single approach to IPT. Harry Stack Sullivan is widely regarded as the pioneer in examining the effect of relationships on functioning. In his view, an infant is fundamentally sociable, with a basic need for both emotional and physical contact. Stack Sullivan sought to make connections between a patient's perceptions of early experiences and current character traits. He sought to elicit interpersonal distortions and unwarranted preconceptions through active interviewing. His counter-transference reactions, speculative interpretations and other provocative means were used in the interview to get a sense of a patient's interpersonal style.

IPT was originally developed as a short-term treatment for depression by Gerald Klerman and Myrna Weissman. There have been other theorists involved in adapting it for personality disorders; Timothy Leary, Lorna Benjamin, Donald Kiesler and Jerry Wiggins.

Benjamin (2003) presents a comprehensive model that takes into consideration behavioral, intrapsychic and social factors. She calls this the **Structural Analysis of Social Behavior** (SASB), providing hypotheses about personality traits and their social origins. As with other interpersonal theorists, she has developed a circumplex, or an organizational circle of personality traits (the example shown is not from Benjamin's work).

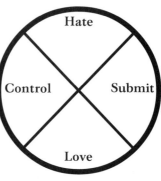

Treatment (interpersonal change) comes about in IPT as a result of several interventions (listed sequentially):

> Increased collaboration between patient and therapist
> ⬇
> Making links between past and current relationships, and the effects the former has on the latter
> ⬇
> Preventing the repetition of self-defeating patterns of interaction
> ⬇
> Motivating patients to abandon destructive patterns
> ⬇
> Facilitating the learning of new ways of interacting

Another facet of IPT involves being aware of what patients hope to accomplish in relationships (**prototypic wishes**):

Antisocial: No one gave me anything but grief, so I seek to take charge and get want I want.

Avoidant: I feel ashamed for the way I am and get embarrassed by my awkwardness, but I do want your acceptance.

Borderline: Being alone means I can be violated again, which I am still angry over, but don't you dare leave me.

Dependent: Anything you want to do is fine, just include me.

Histrionic: Tell me I'm wonderful and you'll always adore me.

Narcissistic: Am I not the best you've ever seen? You should be in awe of my talents, connections and power.

Obsessive-Compulsive: If I show you how perfectly I can do things, then you'll want me around to improve things for you.

Paranoid: You will exploit me as soon as I let down my guard.

Schizoid: Please leave me alone, I am uncomfortable with you.

Schizotypal: Convention has hurt/bored me. There are other ways to explain what goes on around us — let's find them.

A unique facet of IPT is learning the social consequences of expressing affect, neediness or illness. For example, a central theme in borderline personality disorder (BPD) is abandonment and the white-hot anger that ensues when there is even the possibility of being left alone. For example, a BPD patient is faced with having a spouse leave on a business trip which he or she cannot attend. The feeling of panic becomes overwhelming and anger is used to control the spouse into providing the desperately needed nurturance. The patient needs to learn that the anger only serves to distance the spouse and may lead to real abandonment. There are more effective ways of seeking reassurance about being loved than forcing others into a certain role.

3.9   Integrating Therapeutic Strategies

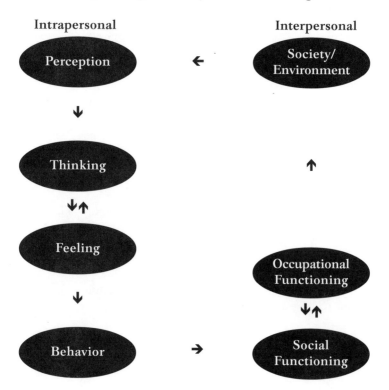

All psychiatric disorders can be considered in terms of aberrations of perception, affective state, cognition and behavior. By virtue of being considered "disorders," these conditions impact on a individual's ability to function at work and in relationships.

In addition to this general scheme, there are specific aspects that apply to personality disorders:
- The **ego defense mechanisms** employed are either primitive or used to an exaggerated extent, however, psychotic defense are not used (i.e. personality disorders are not considered psychotic disorders).
- In order to successfully treat patient with personality disorders, it is often necessary to intervene at as many "entry points" in the above scheme as possible.

3.10   References

American Psychiatric Association
Diagnostic and Statistical Manual of Mental Disorders, 4ᵗʰ Edition, Text Revision
American Psychiatric Association, Arlington, VA, 2000

Beck AT, Freeman A, Davis DD & Associates
Cognitive Therapy of Personality Disorders, 2ⁿᵈ Edition
The Guilford Press, New York, 2003

Benjamin LS
Interpersonal Diagnosis and Treatment of Personality Disorders, 2ⁿᵈ Edition
The Guilford Press, New York, 2003

Bolwby J
Attachment, 2ⁿᵈ Edition
Basic Books, New York, 1983

Campbell RJ
Psychiatric Dictionary, 8ᵗʰ Edition
Oxford University Press, New York, 2004

Erik H. Erikson EH
Identity and the Life Cycle
W.W. Norton, New York, 1994

Gabbard GO
Psychodynamic Psychiatry in Clinical Practice, 4ᵗʰ Edition
American Psychiatric Publishing, Inc., Arlington VA, 2005

Goldstein WN
A Primer for Beginning Psychotherapy
Brunner/Mazel, New York, 1998

Kernberg O
Notes on countertransference.
J. of the American Psychoanalytic Assoc., 13: p.38-56, 1965

Klerman G & Rounsaville B
Interpersonal Psychotherapy of Depression
Basic Books, New York, 1984

Links PS, Editor
Clinical Assessment and Management of Severe Personality Disorders
American Psychiatric Press, Inc., Washington, DC, 1996

Livesley JW, Editor
The DSM-IV Personality Disorders
The Guilford Press, New York, 1995

Mahler MS, Pine F & Bergman A
The Psychological Birth of the Human Infant: Symbiosis and Individuation
Basic Books, New York, 2000

Millon T with Davis RD
Disorders of Personality: DSM-IV and Beyond, Second Edition
Wiley & Sons, Inc, New York, 1996

Mount J
Causation of psychological symptoms.
Personal Communication, 1995 Revision

Piaget J
The Psychology of the Child
Basic Books, New York, 2000

Pies RW
Clinical Manual of Psychiatric Diagnosis and Treatment
American Psychiatric Press, Inc., Washington, DC, 1994

Rutan JS & Stone WN
Psychodynamic Group Psychotherapy, 2nd Edition
The Guilford Press, New York, 1993

Sperry L
Cognitive Behavior Therapy of DSM-IV Personality Disorders
Brunner/Mazel, New York, 1999

Steinberg PI
The Psychodynamic Formulation
Personal Communication, 1995

Vaillant G
Ego Mechanisms of Defense
American Psychiatric Press, Inc., Washington, DC, 1992

Weissman MM & Markowitz JC
Comprehensive Guide to Interpersonal Psychotherapy
Basic Books, New York, 2000

Winnicott DW
Winnicott on the Child
Perseus Press, New York, 2002

Young JE
Cognitive Therapy for Personality Disorders: A Schema Focused Approach, Revised Edition
Practitioner's Resource Press, Sarasota, FL, 1994

Chapter 4

Ego Psychology
&
Ego Defenses

4.1   What is Ego Psychology?

In 1900, Freud published *The Interpretation of Dreams* and developed his **topographical theory**, which divided the mind into the **conscious**, **unconscious**, and **preconscious**. The unconscious mind contains wishes seeking fulfillment that are closely related to instinctual drives, specifically sexual and aggressive urges. A particular type of thinking called **primary process** is associated with the unconscious. Primary process is not bound by logic, permits contradictions to coexist, contains no negatives, has no regard for time, and is highly symbolized. Examples of this type of thinking are seen in dreams, psychosis, and children's logic.

The preconscious is an agency of the mind that develops over time and is involved in the censorship of wishes and desires. It facilitates bi-directional communication between the conscious and unconscious. The preconscious and conscious mind use **secondary process** thinking, which is logical and deals with the demands of external reality. Secondary process is the goal-directed, day-to-day type of thinking used by rational adults.

Over time, Freud noticed that he encountered **resistance** to his therapeutic interventions. He observed that patients defended themselves against the recollection of painful memories. In the topographical model, the preconscious was accessible to consciousness. However, in light of the resistance he was experiencing, he postulated that there was an unconscious aspect of the mind responsible for repressing memories.

Freud incorporated his findings into his **structural theory**, introduced with the publication of *The Ego and the Id* in 1923. This consisted of a tripartite structure containing the **id, ego,** and **superego.** Present from birth, the **id** is completely unconscious and seeks gratification of instinctive (mainly sexual and aggressive) drives. The **superego** forms from an identification with the same-sex parent at the resolution of the **oedipal conflict.** It suppresses instinctual aims, serves as the moral conscience in dictating what should not be done, and as the ego ideal, dictates what should be done. The superego is largely unconscious, but has a conscious element.

The ego is the mediator between the id and superego, and between the person and reality. The ego has both conscious and unconscious elements. The following are considered the conscious roles of the ego:
- Perception (sense of reality)
- Reality testing (adaptation to reality)
- Motor control
- Intuition
- Memory
- Affect (visibly expressed emotion)
- Thinking (the ego uses secondary process) and Learning
- Control of instinctual drives (delay of immediate gratification)
- Synthetic functions (assimilation, creation, coordination)
- Language and comprehension

The fundamental concept in ego psychology is one of conflict between these three agencies. The **id, ego,** and **superego** battle for expression and discharge of sexual and aggressive drives. This conflict produces anxiety, specifically called **signal anxiety.** This anxiety alerts the ego that **defense mechanisms** are required, which is an unconscious role of the ego. The events can be conceptualized as follows:

The id seeks expression of an impulse
⬇
The superego prohibits the impulse from being expressed
⬇
This conflict produces signal anxiety
⬇
An ego defense is unconsciously recruited
to decrease the anxiety
⬇
Repression is the first defense used; others follow if required
⬇
A character trait or neurotic symptom is formed
based in part on which other ego defenses are used

The consequence of an ego defense can be thought of as a compromise which allows expression of the impulse in a disguised form. Such compromise formations can be part of adaptive mental functioning. However, when such compromises are pathological they are considered neurotic symptoms. Everyone, normal or neurotic, employs a repertoire of defense mechanisms in varying degrees. All defenses protect the ego from the instinctive drives of the id, and are generally unconscious processes.

Freud directed most of his attention to **repression,** which he considered the primary ego defense. Repression is defined as the expelling and withholding of an idea or feeling from conscious awareness. He thought other defenses were used only when repression failed to diminish the anxiety. Freud's daughter, Anna, described nine defense mechanisms in her 1936 book, *The Ego and the Mechanisms of Defense.* Since then, more defense mechanisms have been identified. Akin to the theories of life cycle development, there is a progression in the use of ego defenses with maturity.

> **Important Properties of Ego Defenses**
> 1. Defenses are a major means of managing instinct and affect.
> 2. Ego defenses are unconscious mechanisms.
> 3. Ego defenses are discrete from each other.
> 4. Ego defenses can by dynamic and reversible
> 5. Ego defenses are often the hallmarks of major psychiatric syndromes
> 6. Ego defenses can be adaptive as well as pathological
> Source: Adapted from Vaillant (1992)

4.2 Classification of Ego Defenses

George Vaillant (1992) catalogued defenses into four categories: **narcissistic, immature, neurotic,** and **mature.** Fuller explanations of these defenses can be found in his writings and other reference texts. The key defenses found in personality disorders are presented in the next section of this chapter.

Narcissistic Defenses
Denial
Distortion
Primitive Idealization
Projection
Projective Identification
Splitting

Neurotic Defenses
Controlling
Displacement
Dissociation
Externalization
Inhibition
Intellectualization
Isolation
Rationalization
Reaction Formation
Repression
Sexualization
Undoing

Mature Defenses
Altruism
Anticipation
Asceticism
Humor
Sublimation
Suppression

Immature Defenses
Acting Out
Blocking
Hypochondriasis
Identification
Introjection
Passive-Aggressive Behavior
Projection
Regression
Schizoid Fantasy
Somatization

4.3   Mnemonic for Ego Defenses
"BUD HAS PRICE" *

Blocking
Undoing
Displacement, Denial, Distortion, Dissociation

Hypochondriasis, Humor
Acting Out, Altruism, Anticipation, Asceticism
Sublimation, Suppression, Schizoid Fantasy, Somatization

Projection, Projective Identification, Passive-Aggressive Behavior,
    Primitive Idealization
Rationalization, Reaction Formation, Repression, Regression
Identification, Idealization, Introjection, Inhibition,
    Intellectualization, Isolation of Affect
Controlling
Externalization

* From the book:

*Mnemonics & More
for Psychiatry*

David J. Robinson, MD

© Rapid Psychler Press

4.4 Ego Defenses in Personality Disorders

An understanding of defensive mechanisms is essential for recognizing and treating Axis II disorders. *"Understanding the defenses of another person allows us to empathize rather than condemn, to understand rather than dismiss."* (Vaillant, 1992)

Personalities become "disordered" by the maladaptive use of ego defenses, both in terms of which defenses are used and to the extent that they are used. The major defenses seen in use by the different personality disorders are as follows:

Antisocial: Acting Out, Controlling, Dissociation, Projective Identification

Avoidant: Displacement, Inhibition, Isolation, Projection

Borderline: Acting Out, Dissociation, Distortion, Projective Identification, Splitting

Dependent: Idealization, Inhibition, Projective Identification, Reaction Formation, Regression, Somatization

Histrionic: Denial, Regression, Dissociation, Repression, Sexualization

Narcissistic: Identification, Idealization/Devaluation, Projection

Obsessive-Compulsive: Displacement, Intellectualization, Isolation of Affect, Rationalization, Reaction Formation, Undoing

Paranoid: Denial, Projection, Projective Identification, Reaction Formation, Splitting

Schizoid: Idealization/Devaluation, Intellectualization, Introjection, Projection, Schizoid Fantasy

Schizotypal: Denial, Distortion, Idealization, Projection, Schizoid Fantasy

4.5 Ego Defenses Illustrated

Repression is considered to be the principal ego defense and therefore receives a large drawing. Repression is an active process that excludes distressing material from conscious awareness. Freud thought this was integral to the formation of psychological symptoms. The "distressing material" can be further defined as consisting of three things: an instinctual impulse, an idea, and the accompanying emotion or affect. For an example, let's get Oedipal. A boy may consciously be aware of hating his father, an idea and emotion which are both too upsetting to bear. If the idea re-enters consciousness, it is altered so that rather than the father being hated, a substitute chosen (such as another authority figure). In this way, what is forgotten is not forgotten, and the object of the strong feelings is symbolically linked to the original conflict.

Primary Repression refers to stopping an idea or affect before it reaches consciousness.

Secondary Repression removes from consciousness what was once experienced.

Suppression is the conscious avoidance of attending to an impulse or conflict.

As an example, primary repression would involve not reading this book in the first place. Secondary repression would be reading it and then forgetting what was presented. Suppression would be consciously avoiding this book because it reminds you of an unpleasant event (like an examination).

Acting Out

Acting out is the expression of an unconscious impulse through behavior in order to avoid experiencing the accompanying painful feelings. The action provides partial gratification of the wish rather than prohibition against it. For example, as a patient in psychotherapy nears the end of treatment, unconscious fears of abandonment arise (which stem from previous relationships). The patient may then "act out" these feelings of abandonment by taking an overdose instead of dealing with the pain of feeling rejected. The action serves as a substitute for remembering and is an unrecognized (unconscious) repetition of earlier behavior. Acting out involves more than a single thought or behavior. The term is properly used to describe an inappropriate response to a current situation as if it were the original conflict. The term is often improperly used to describe conscious, impulsive behavior, which is more accurately called **acting up** or **misbehaving** (as the fellow on the right is demonstrating).

Controlling

Controlling is the unconscious manipulation of events, people, or objects in the environment to serve an inner need, such as the reduction of tension or lessening the anxiety that accompanies a conflict

Denial

In this defense reality is simply ignored. Painful affects or memories are avoided by the disavowal of sensory input. Denial can be a primitive defense, but also has adaptive elements, such as helping patients cope with serious conditions or dealing with upsetting events.

Displacement

Displacement transfers the emotion attached to a conflicted wish or troubled relationship to an avenue where expression of strong feelings is permitted, more acceptable, or at least is less forbidden. Common examples are "kicking the dog" or "shooting the messenger." The target of the discharge remains symbolically linked to the original source of the conflict.

Dissociation

Dissociation is the sudden and drastic alteration of an aspect of consciousness, identity, or behavior. It is a temporary state which allows the person to avoid emotional distress.

Distortion

This involves altering one's perception of the environment by replacing reality with a more acceptable version in order to suit one's inner needs. The degree of distortion can be mild or can be so severe that psychosis develops.

Idealization/Devaluation

In idealization, exceedingly positive qualities are ascribed to another person (or the idea/mental image of that person). The beauty, strength, skill, unconditional love, etc. attributed to that person is unrealistic. Typically, the object of the idealization demonstrates the desirable qualities to some extent, and is someone who can provide comfort, assistance, empathy, etc., but not to the (unrealistic) level desired. If such wishes are met to a certain extent it serves only to increase expectations. This escalates to the point where the idealized person cannot possibly meet the spiraling expectations. Inevitably, disappointment results, whereby the idealized person is vilified far out of proportion to the actual "failure," but not according to the extreme wishes of the idealizee.

A common example of this is the hero worship lavished on movie stars or athletes. They can do no wrong until they snub you for an autograph or don't reply to your tenth fan letter, at that point in time they may well become objects of contempt.

Identification

In this defense mechanism, patients adopt some, many, or all of the characteristics of another person as their own. As an example, this mechanism is familiar in the marketing of sports equipment such that the buyer identifies with the professionals who use the same brand. This effect usually lasts until the first use of the items.

Inhibition

Inhibition is an unconscious confinement, restraining or checking of instinctual impulses. The superego prevents the expression of the impulse from the id. This has also been described as a conscious mechanism which serves the similar purpose of helping avoid expression of the conflicted wish which would cause problems with the superego (conscience) and/or other people.

Intellectualization

This defense involves the extreme or exclusive use of "thinking" to deal with emotional issues. This has also been referred to as a "thinking compulsion." Attention is focused on external matters, inanimate objects, or irrelevant details in order to avoid intimacy. Expression of emotion is restricted or absent. This is present in an unempathic "just deal with it" attitude, and is a component of brooding where events are continually rehashed in a distant, abstract, emotionally barren fashion.

Introjection

Introjection is the internalizing of the characteristics of another person in order to feel a constant connection with that individual. In cases where the other person is loved, introjection helps in maintaining a consistent sense of closeness. Introjection can also operate where the other person is feared. In these situations, it places aggression under one's control instead of the feeling that it arises from elsewhere. Some degree of introjection is a vital aspect of normal development. In contrast to identification, introjection is a more automatic, cohesive process that doesn't significantly alter a person's sense of him or herself.

Isolation of Affect

This defense, which is also called simply isolation, involves the separation of an idea and its accompanying affect. The affect is subsequently kept out of conscious awareness. The idea, stripped of its emotional charge, is more easily dealt with on a conscious level.

Passive-Aggression

Passive-aggressive behavior is the expression of hostile feelings in a non-confrontational manner. Examples are lateness, procrastination, telling partial truths, and acts of omission rather than commission that obstruct others. Both the passive and aggressive elements are expressed simultaneously. This term was applied to a discrete personality disorder in DSM-III-R (it was deleted presumably because these forms of behavior are so common they can't rightfully be considered a disorder).

Projection

Projection involves the casting out or a "projecting" onto others the thoughts or feelings which the person cannot tolerate as being his or her own. In the example below, the man with the glasses blames his wife for having an affair with the elderly gentleman, when he himself has been harboring yearnings for another woman. This can also be summed up as, "a good defense starts with a good offense." By blaming others for their sentiments and actions, the focus stays away from the person making the accusations.

Projective Identification

Projective identification is a difficult defense to conceptualize. An analogy is that of a self-fulfilling prophecy. Unwanted aspects of the self are projected onto others, and in a way that fits the person on whom they are projected. In the illustration that follows, the patient can't tolerate inner feelings of being unlikable, so via projection, the therapist is accused of hating her. This projection is "reasonable" because some patients are difficult to work with, and in this instance there may have been something that occurred to make the patient feel rejected. The patient then exerts unconscious interpersonal pressure on the therapist to think, feel, and act in a way that is in accordance with projection. This is the identification aspect. Finally, once this projection is "processed" by the therapist, it is re-internalized by the patient, and in this case, she becomes the difficult patient she said she was at the outset. This defense is effective in making others feel what the person herself is experiencing.

If we consider the unconscious communication (meta-messages, subspace channels, etc.) between a patient and therapist, an example of this defense can also be illustrated as follows:

Patient: *"I have only ever known people who were abusive and neglectful, and I believe that you will treat me this way as well. I am going to project onto you my fears."* (shown by throwing darts)

Patient: *"Are you neglectful? Incompetent? Insecure?"*
Therapist: *"No."*
Patient: *"Are you abusive?*
Therapist: *"I can be if I am provoked with the right taunts."*

Patient: *"I am going to provoke you by being late, calling you at home, and criticizing you. I will make you abusive towards me, just like everyone else has been."*

Rationalization

Rationalization is the process of covering up unreasonable or unacceptable behaviors or ideas with seemingly reasonable explanations. Justification is provided for beliefs or behaviors that would otherwise appear illogical, irrational, or immoral.

Reaction Formation

In this defense, unacceptable wishes are transformed into their complete opposite. This has also been called **reversal formation**, and can be thought of as socializing the infantile urges that persist on an unconscious level.

Regression

Regression involves the return to a previous (lower) level of functioning, which can serve the purpose conflict avoidance. It is easier to find gratification at earlier stages of development, as well as having fewer responsibilities. This can be seen to an extent in most inpatients who because of the illness cannot maintain their usual level of function, and have fewer expectations placed on them while in hospital.

Schizoid Fantasy

Fantasy is used as a escape and a means of gratification as others are not required for fulfillment. The retreat into fantasy itself acts as a means of distancing others.

Sexualization

Objects, situations, and people are colored with sexual overtones that were either not there initially, or if present were subtle. This can help lessen anxiety by reducing everything to a base level, or assigning a common element to unknown or uncomfortable situations.

Somatization

In this defense, psychological difficulties become expressed as physical complaints. There is also a major psychiatric condition (Axis I) called **somatization disorder.** Somatization is considered a form of regression because expressing emotional problems verbally is developmental progress. Some family situations and cultures encourage somatization by reducing the attention paid to emotional concerns, thereby facilitating their expression in physical terms.

Splitting

This defense divides people or situations into "all good" or "all bad" categories. Ambivalence towards the people or situations cannot be tolerated. Rapid shifts between the good and bad categories occurs, with little to no recall of the previous concept or an awareness of the self-contradictory switch. Splitting can be directed towards a single person, group of people, institutions, etc. Often only a minor or even symbolic event invokes a shift in the split.

Undoing

Undoing is an action instead of a psychological mechanism. The ensuing behavior is linked to a conflict, and is carried out to prevent or reverse the consequences that are anticipated from taking action (such as acting on an impulse). Undoing can be realistically or magically associated with the conflict and serves to reduce anxiety and control the underlying impulse.

4.6   Mature Ego Defenses

The preceding section is not a comprehensive presentation of ego defenses, but an introduction to those that are relevant for an introduction to personality disorders. Keep in mind that defense mechanisms are used by everyone because defenses do have adaptive elements. For example, some patients with terminal illnesses fare better by denying their condition (to a certain extent), and getting the most out of their lives. Regression is an essential ingredient in creativity, and the term **regression in service of the ego** refers to instances where it is beneficial to allow one's self to enjoy a less demanding situation or experience. Mature ego defenses allow the expression of impulses in socially acceptable ways.

Anticipation

Anticipation involves the postponement of wishes or impulses until they can be more appropriately expressed. Discomfort may result from deferring action, but satisfaction is achieved from avoiding unpleasant outcomes.

Humor

Humor is the expression of feelings in a manner that causes neither personal discomfort nor is unpleasant to others. It allows one to focus on issues that are difficult or unpleasant to bear. Freud had many theories about humor, but it appears that it is the "hidden, aggressive wish" proposal that most people remember from his work. A more balanced view is summed up by Elliott Oring, *"Humor is one of the basic languages of intimacy and affection. Those who would reduce humor to disguised expressions of hostility and aggression might well ponder whether humor might not serve to mask expressions of love and tenderness as well."*

Sublimation

This defense allows the channeling of aggressive impulses towards a modified outlet. Playing sports is an example of sublimation.

4.7 References

Freud A
The Ego and the Mechanisms of Defense
Hogarth Press, London, England, 1936

Freud S
Jokes and Their Relation to the Unconscious
The Interpretation of Dreams, in
The Standard Edition of the Complete Psychological Works of Sigmund Freud,
Strachey, J, Editor
Hogarth Press, London, England, 1960

Freud S
The Ego and the Id
W.W. Norton, Co., New York, 1960

Gabbard GO
Psychodynamic Psychiatry in Clinical Practice, 4ᵗʰ Ed.
American Psychiatric Press, Inc., Arlington, VA, 2005

Greenspan SI
The development of the ego: biological and environmental specificity in
the psychopathological developmental process and the selection and
construction of ego defenses.
J Am Psychoanal Assoc. 37(3): p. 605-38, 1989

Karasu TB
A developmental metatheory of psychopathology.
Am J Psychother. 48(4): p. 581-99 , Fall 1994

Mulder RT, Joyce PR, Sellman JD, Sullivan PF, Cloninger CR
Towards an understanding of defense style in terms of temperament and
character.
Acta Psychiatr Scand. 93(2): p. 99-104, 1996

Nesse RM
The evolutionary functions of repression and the ego defenses.
J Am Acad Psychoanal. 18(2): p. 260-85, Summer 1990

Oring E
Jokes and Their Relations
University of Kentucky Press, Lexington, Kentucky, 1992

Vaillant GE
Ego Mechanisms of Defense: A Guide for Clinicians and Researchers
American Psychiatric Press, Inc., Washington DC, 1992

Vaillant GE
Ego mechanisms of defense and personality psychopathology.
J Abn Psychol. 103(1): p. 44-50, 1994

Chapter 5

Biological Dimensions

5.1   What Does "Psychosomatic" Mean?

Despite the relatively recent use of the term psychosomatic, the concept of a reciprocal relationship between the health of the mind and the health of the body has existed since antiquity. Ancient societies appreciated the presence of a cause-and-effect relationship between mind and body. Illnesses were deemed to involve social and emotional factors and often thought to have magical or religious origins. Accordingly, efforts to treat diseases were largely based on such beliefs and the faith that the afflicted person had in the spiritual healer. The power invested by society in such shamans, as well as their personal qualities, were the curative factors in these relationships.

Psychosomatic

Psychosomatic medicine is concerned "holistically" with the whole patient — the effects of the mind on the body and vice versa.

Psyche	**Soma**
The study of the psyche became divided — the "mind" by philosophers and the "soul" by theologians. The emotional aspects of illness (both causing and being the result of physical illnesses) lack objective findings, and are seen as unscientific because of the high degree of variablity from person to person.	Virchow, the founder of modern pathology, stated that *"disease has its origin in disease of the cell"* in that: • Subcellular components are affected by disease, altering cellular function and eventually structure • Tissue and organ changes are observable on a microscopic and macroscopic level.

With the disintegration of ancient Greek and Roman civilizations, the concept of illness reverted back to causation resulting from personal, societal or spiritual causes. Religious causes in particular were considered the dominant factor in the etiology of illness (i.e. sinning). Until the Renaissance, religious figures were the ones principally involved in treating sickness.

Eventually, the advances made in other scientific fields led to the discovery that certain illnesses had demonstrable organic findings. Autopsies revealed that tissue and organ changes, rather than those in the spiritual realm, caused or were associated with diseases. The use of the microscope detected pathological changes on a cellular level. This started an era where the causes for illnesses were elucidated, the pathological findings correlated and remedies sought, which shifted medicine's focus to treating the illness instead of the patient.

Freud, a neurologist by training, worked with Charcot in Paris. This gave him first-hand experience with hysteria, a condition in which Charcot was especially interested. Freud observed that hypnotic suggestion could cause hysterical (physical) manifestations, and this started him thinking about hysteria having a psychological origin. He had developed a special interest in linking hypnosis and neurology, and ultimately psychology to neurophysiology.

The terms **psychosomatic** and **psychosomatic medicine** still carry considerable ambiguity. Lipowski (1984) traced the historical references and uses of these terms, and offers the following definitions:
- *Psychosomatic* — refers to the inseparability and interdependence of psychosocial and biologic (physiologic) aspects of humankind
- *Psychosomatic medicine* — refers to the discipline concerned with: a) the study of the correlations of psychological functions, normal or pathologic, and of the interplay of biologic and psychosocial factors in the development, course, and outcome of diseases; and b) advocacy of a holistic (or biopsychosocial) approach to patient care and application of methods derived from behavioral sciences to prevention and treatment.

Lipowski stresses that there have been two enduring aspects of psychosomatic medicine:

- The holistic conception — which refers to the treatment of the whole patient by focusing on emotional/psychological factors in addition to the somatic/physiologic (this is contained in the definition of psychosomatic)
- The psychogenic conception — which refers to the mental or psychological etiology of an illness

5.2 What is the Biopsychosocial Model?

As an application of psychosomatic principles, Engel (1967, 1977) published an integrated approach to understanding the multi-factorial influences on the causation and course of illnesses. A balanced and comprehensive view of the etiology (also called a **formulation**) and treatment of illnesses can be made using this model:

	Biological	Psychological	Social
Predisposing			
Precipitating			
Perpetuating			
Protective			

Some of these factors are intuitively obvious. Physical illness, by definition, has biological aberrations. For example, cirrhosis or Alzheimer's disease has characteristic pathologic findings in the liver and brain cells, respectively. However, there are psychosocial factors involved in medical illnesses, such as the issue of stress (Type A personalities) in heart disease or emotional upset and its relation to exacerbations of psoriasis.

Psychiatric disorders are still often referred to as "functional" in that no "organic" impairment has been consistently demonstrated. Nevertheless, there are many biological aspects to mental illnesses. This ranges from conditions which are clearly genetically based (e.g. psychosis in Wilson's disease, which is an inherited defect in copper metabolism) to those that are more speculative, such as mild birth anoxia. Many Axis I conditions are now being found to have genetic associations (e.g. genes associated with bipolar mood disorder are thought to be on chromosomes 5, 11 and X). There are also physical findings associated with many major psychiatric disorders, for example:

- Smooth pursuit eye movement abnormalities in schizophrenia
- Endocrine and sleep abnormalities in depression
- Metabolic irregularities in certain brain regions in patients with obsessive-compulsive disorder
- The majority of patients presenting with a conversion disorder go on to develop bona fide neurological disorders within several years

5.3   The Biopsychosocial Management Plan

A comprehensive management plan for psychiatric conditions is included on the following pages. While this is a comprehensive plan designed to address the salient parameters for Axis I conditions, many of these factors apply to patients with severe personality disorders (who are frequently hospitalized) and patients who have personality changes induced by physical illnesses, substance use or the side-effects of medications or other treatments.

Investigations

Biological

- Admission physical exam
- Diagnostic tests:
  - *Routine*: hematologic and clinical chemistry admission/screening bloodwork
  - *Toxicology*: serum medication levels; urine screen for substances of abuse
  - *Special assays*
- Diagnostic investigations: CXR, EKG
- Neuroimaging: CT, MRI scans
- EEG
- Consultations to other medical/surgical specialties
- Special tests:
  - *hypothalamic/pituitary/adrenal axis testing* (DST, TRH stimulation test, GH response)
  - *sleep studies*

Social

- Collateral history:
  - *Friends and family members*
  - *Primary care physician*
  - *Community psychiatrist*
  - *Other clinics, programs or hospitals*
- Activities of Daily Living (ADL) assessment
- Referral to members of interdisciplinary team
  - *Social Worker*
  - *Occupational Therapist*
  - *Physiotherapist*
  - *Dietician/Nutritional Counselor*
  - *Clergy*
  - *Nurse Clinician*

Psychological

- Psychometric testing
- Cognitive screening tests (e.g. *Mini-Mental State Exam, Clock Drawing*, etc.)
- Neuropsychological test batteries
- Structured interviews/diagnostic testing

Treatment — Short Term

Biological

- Psychpharmacology
    Antidepressants, Mood Stabilizers
    Antipsychotics, Antiparkinsonian Agents
    Anxiolytics, Sedative-Hypnotics, Psychostimulants
    Others
- ECT
- Other psychiatric treatments
- Address somatic illnesses
    Medications, Physical Treatments
- Detoxification from medications or substances
- Environmental
    Level of observation/Seclusion Room/Passes
    Attire (pyjamas or street clothes)
    Mechanical restraints

Social

- Social services/Family meetings
    Assistance with housing, finances, etc.
- Education and focus/support groups
- Occupational Therapy
- Administrative
    Voluntary/Involuntary Status
    Rights/Legal Advice
    Duty to Warn or Duty to Protect Others
    Treatment Contracts
    Informing work/school of absence
    Obtaining consent if patient incapable

Psychological

- Advice/Reality Therapy
- Behavior Therapy/Modification
- Cognitive Therapy
- Group Therapy
- Milieu Therapy
- Recreation Therapy
- Stress Management/Coping Skills
- Other therapies with a shorter-term focus

Treatment — Longer Term

Biological

- Reduction/optimization of dosage
- Depot antipsychotic medications
- Monitoring vulnerable organ systems
- Serum level monitoring
- Adjunct/augmentation/combination treatments
- Reducing factors affecting efficacy of medication
    Nicotine
    Caffeine
    Liver enzyme inducers
    Others
- Health teaching and lifestyle changes

Social

- Vocational rehabilitation
- Religious/Spiritual guidance
- Community supports and organizations
- Discharge planning
    Transfer to another facility
    Housing considerations
    Case Manager/Management
- Liaison with Primary Care Provider

Psychological

- Psychotherapy
    Continuation of inpatient therapy
    Arrange outpatient treatment
- Match various types of therapies to needs and
    Attainable goals for the patient
- Skills Training

Comprehensive Management Parameters

	Biological	Psychological	Social
Investigations			
Short-Term Treatment			
Longer-Term Treatment			

5.4 Biology and Personality

The concordance rate for schizophrenia in monozygotic (identical) twins is about fifty percent. Put another way, when one twin develops this illness, the other will only do so half the time. This condition exists as a paradigm in psychiatry for a condition where biological and psychosocial influences are equally important.

Loehlin (1982) has shown that personality traits (not disorders) also have an inheritance on the order of fifty percent. Thus, biochemical forces in the form of hormones, neurotransmitters and many other compounds exert an important effect on mental processes. In order to further examine the biological dimension of personality, **temperament** and **character** must be differentiated:

Temperament	Character
Temperament is the genetic or constitutional contribution to personality. It refers to an individual's inherited disposition to feel, act, and think in specific, restricted ways.	Character is derived from the Greek word for "engraving." It refers to the distinctive qualities of a person that are learned or develop through socialization and experience.

Personality
Personality is considered a blend of temperamental and characterological factors.

Temperament and character can be further distinguished by the two long-term memory systems, procedural and declerative:

Procedural	Declerative
• involves the cortico-striatal regions of the brain	• involves the cortico-limbic-diencephalic regions of the brain
• preverbal (presemantic) processing of perceptions	• experiences are represented as words, images and symbols
• visuospatial and emotional aspects are stored here	• these memories are factual, can be consciously retreived, expressed verbally and lead to intentional action
• can operative independently of declarative memory	
• called "knowing how" memory	• called "knowing what" memory
• **unconscious/instinctive**	• **conscious/uses reason**

Character development is concerned with learned psychosocial influences, socialization and how basic beliefs or a concept of self is formed. Character is often referred to in terms of Freud's psychosexual stages (oral, anal, etc.) or in terms of which ego defense mechanisms are thought to be operative. Character is considered to be ingrained with declerative memory and temperament with procedural memory, where it is processed on an unconscious, pre-conceptual level. Temperamental factors are considered heritable and are manifested before significant learning occurs. Chess & Thomas (1986), Sigvardsson (1987) and Kagan (1988) have shown that temperamental traits range from moderately to substantially predictive of behavior/personality style later in life.

Establishing core temperamental factors is a subject of intense research and debate. Chess & Thomas (1986) identified nine autonomic reactions in the behaviors of infants:
- Activity level — degree of motor behavior
- Adaptability — facility with which behavior is modified to match changes in the environment
- Approach or withdrawal — quality of the response to new stimuli
- Attention span and persistence — length of time engaged in an activity and the degree of continuation when faced with obstacles
- Distractibility — degree to which extraneous stimuli divert attention
- Intensity of reaction —degree to which emotions are expressed
- Quality of mood — degree of socially engaging behavior
- Rhythmicity — the stability of cyclical behaviors, such as sleeping, eating, elimination, etc.
- Threshold of responsiveness — the minimum level of stimulation required to evoke a reaction

Most other authors identify between three and seven temperamental factors, with **five factor models** being the most popular. Eysenck & Eysenck (1976) identify three dimensions of temperament: **neuroticism, extraversion-introversion** and **psychoticism.** Instead of psychoticism, Tellengen (1985) suggested **constraint** and Costa & McCrae (1992) proposed openness to experience. **Conscientousness** and **agreeableness** are also frequently included in five-factor models.

Cloninger (1987) identified three main dimensions to temperament: **novelty seeking, harm avoidance,** and **reward dependence,** later adding **persistence** as a fourth quality in Cloninger (1993). Costello (1996) added aggressiveness and behavioral inhibition to this list. Of those contributing to the understanding of temperament, Cloninger (1987) argues that while DSM-IV-TR considers the five different axes, it has the following shortcomings regarding personality disorders:

• Often more than one diagnosis is applicable
• There is an arbitrary division made between style and disorder
• The behaviors listed in the diagnostic criteria, in general, are socially undesirable, so defensiveness and minimization are common

Even among individuals with some insight into the effects of their actions, it can be difficult to get valid information to make a diagnosis. Because these disorders are **egosyntonic,** and the locus of responsibility is often seen as being outside of the person, researchers continually seek more direct, standardized methods of assessment applicable across cultures. Cloninger sought temperamental factors that are biologically independent, span the range from adaptive to pathological, and have an application to current diagnostic nosology. For example, the factors involved in the **Millon Clinical Multiaxial Inventory (MCMI)** are: negativistic-avoidant, asocial-avoidant, and paranoid, which do not exist on a continuum with adaptive traits. Many inventories use three variables to describe personality variation, Cloninger's (1987) are:

• **Harm Avoidance** — an inherited response that inhibits behavior leading would lead to punishment, novel situations or frustration.

- **Novelty Seeking** — an innate tendency involving exploratory activity leading to exhilaration or other rewards, or behavior that reduces drudgery, monotony or punishment.

- **Reward Dependence** — the constitutional tendency to respond to rewarding situations and to maintain behaviors that continue gratification or bring some relief from punishment.

Cloninger also suggested that the above sequence represents a phylogeny of temperamental factors in that harm avoidance is a basic quality in all animals. With more evolved species comes novelty seeking and then reward dependence, which maintains key behaviors. These temperamental factors can be described as follows:

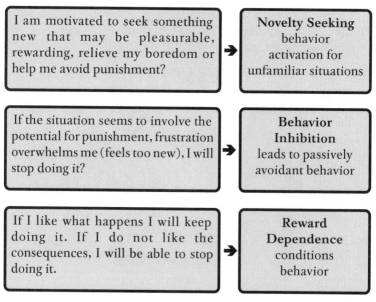

Cloninger developed detailed descriptions for each of these three dimensions that were scored on a seven-point scale:

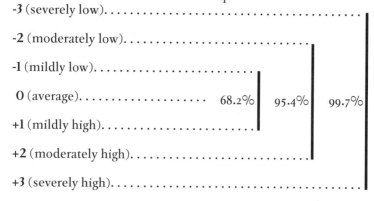

-3 (severely low)...

-2 (moderately low)...

-1 (mildly low)...

0 (average)....................... 68.2%   95.4%   99.7%

+1 (mildly high).......................................

+2 (moderately high)...

+3 (severely high)...

Cloninger's rating system corresponds with standard scores on a Gaussian distribution. He was able to demonstrate that these three dimensions are independent, and allow for a flexible an integrated pattern of response to varying conditions of novelty, reward and punishment. Cloninger set up a third grid with high and low aspects of each dimension. Then, personality characteristics were derived from blending or the intersection of temperamental dimensions (e.g.

being impulsive is an amalgamation of high novelty seeking and low harm avoidance):

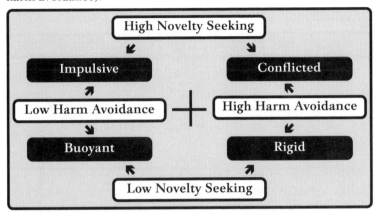

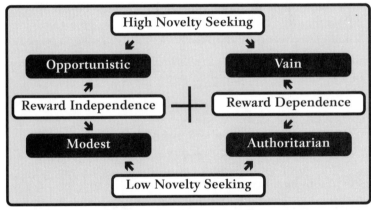

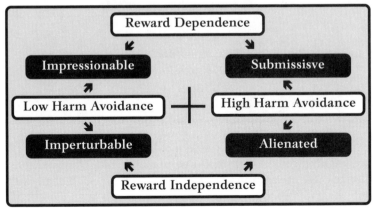

Personality characteristics/behaviors can then be correlated with DSM-IV-TR diagnoses by amalgamating the "corners" or intersections of the preceding three diagrams:

- **Antisocial Personality Disorder**
  Impulsive, Opportunistic, Imperturbable
  Novelty Seeking — high, Harm Avoidance — low, Reward Dependence — low

- **Dependent Personality Disorder & Avoidant Personality Disorder**
  Rigid, Authoritarian, Submissive
  Novelty Seeking — low, Harm Avoidance — high, Reward Dependence — high

- **Histrionic Personality Disorder, Borderline Personality Disorder & Narcissisitic Personality Disorder**
  Impulsive, Vain, Impressionable
  Novelty Seeking — high, Harm Avoidance — low, Reward Dependence — high

- **Obsessive-Compulsive Personality Disorder**
  Rigid, Modest, Alienated
  Novelty Seeking — low, Harm Avoidance — high, Reward Dependence — low

- **Schizoid Personality Disorder**
  Buoyant, Modest, Imperturbable
  Novelty Seeking — low, Harm Avoidance — low, Reward Dependence — low

- **Schizotypal Personality Disorder**
  Buoyant, Authoritarian, Impressionable
  Novelty Seeking — low, Harm Avoidance — low, Reward Dependence — high

This scheme does an impressive job of categorizing DSM-IV-TR personality disorders with only three temperamental characteristics, though there are clear limitations in this example. First of all, with only three variables, a maximum of eight disorders can be described.

In Cloninger's article, he included two that were not presented here (the passive-aggressive and explosive personality disorders) because they are not in DSM-IV-TR. Next, he used descriptions of up to seven characteristics for each of the interactions (corners) between the temperament dimensions (this was not done here because of space limitations). No formulation was provided in Cloninger's article for the schizotypal or paranoid personality disorders, which he felt were not extreme variants of personality traits but instead were related to psychotic disorders. Finally, this scheme is not able to clearly differentiate between some of the disorders that fall in the same cluster (such as the avoidant and dependent personalities from Cluster C).

Revising this three-factor model, Cloninger (1993) established persistence as a fourth temperamental factor, defined as perseverance in the face of frustration and fatigue. Perseverance was initially formulated as an aspect of reward dependence, but emerged as an independent factor.

In order to develop a model that formulated distinctions both between personality disorders, and as being distinct from Axis I disorders, Cloninger derived a seven-factor model that considers the above four temperament dimensions and three dimensions of character:

- **Cooperativeness** — acceptance of other people and the willingness to assist them in achieving their goals without selfish domination
- **Self-directedness** — the intentional drive of an individual to commit to a goal or value and to regulate or adapt behavior in accordance with achieving this aim
- **Self-transcendence** — seeing the unity or totality of a situation and one's part its evolution; spirituality and a union with nature

Cloninger found that common to all the personality disorders were low degrees of self-directedness and cooperation, though these were not as helpful in distinguishing between disorders. Self-transcendence was not as sensitive in establishing the presence of a personality disorder, but was helpful in distinguishing schizotypal (high transcendence) from schizoid personality disorder (low transcendence).

An instrument was developed to test the validity of these constructs called the **Temperament & Character Inventory (TCI)**. This is a self-report, true-false questionnaire consisting of 226 items; 107 questions divided among the four temperament dimensions and 119 measuring the three character dimensions. The results support the above described dimensions, and an application of the seven-factor model for diagnosing personality disorders is presented in Svrakic (1993).

Akin the hierarchy of temperamental factors, the three character factors can be considered progressing in development as follows:
• Cooperativeness — identification as part of a society
• Self-directedness — identification as an individual
• Self-transcendence — identification as part of a larger order

Cloninger concludes by speculating that there are genetic factors that are as important in character development as they are in temperament. This can help explain the variation seen between individuals who persist with maladaptive behaviors and those who are able to change them.

5.5   Addressing Temperament in Treatment

The work of Cloninger and others has provided convincing evidence to support the hypothesis that personality development may be hierarchical, and consisting of temperament and character dimensions, which are thought to involve different memory systems. Temperament is most strongly influenced by genetic determinants of behavior, while character is shaped more by experience. Character can be considered a rational, cognitive or schema-based dimension. In contrast, temperament involves processes that are more automated such as perception and habits.

Returning again to the main goals of treatment:
• Symptom reduction
• Improvement in social and occupational functioning
• Effecting a change in the way a person responds to their environment

the last point can be subdivided into targeting character and temperament dimensions.

Many psychotherapies focus specifically on aspects of character. For example, Cloninger's three character factors are addressed by the following types of therapy:
- Self-directedness — psychodynamic psychotherapy, cognitive therapy
- Cooperativeness — interpersonal psychotherapy, Rogerian counseling
- Self-transcendence — Jungian analysis, meditation

Freeman & Davison (1997), Sperry (1999) and other authors herald a paradigm shift in the treatment of personality disorders to focus on both character and temperament dimensions. Furthermore, dyregulation in temperament and coping skills may well need to be addressed before dimensions of character can be treated.

For example, patients with a moderate-to-severe borderline personality disorder frequently manifest the following behaviors:
- Self-mutilation, suicidal gestures and attempts
- Shoplifting and other impulsive acts
- Substance abuse and other self-damaging acts
- Intense but brief relationships which can include promiscuity
- Pervasive moodiness with abrupt shifts lacking clear precipitants

These patients manifest dysregulation of temperamental factors more prominently than those of character. While both aspects require treatment, the temperamental factors would impair or prohibit therapy aimed only at character issues. Specifically, these patients need to curb their tendency to action (impulsivity), control their emotional rollercoasters (unmodulated affect) and become aware how their behavior affects others. Put another way, they must first stop acting out their difficulties before deeper issues (e.g. neglect, abuse, trauma) can be dealt with.

A simplified way of delineating treatment is that psychodynamic and cognitive therapies address *character* dimensions and behavioral therapies (skills training) are geared towards *temperament* dimensions.

A list of treatments for temperamental dysregulation is as follows:

- **Emotional Expression Aspects**
  Too much
  Anger Management Training
  Anxiety Management Training
  Distress Tolerance Training
  Emotional Regulation Training
  Impulse Control Training
  Sensitivity Reduction Training

  Too little
  Empathy Training

  Identification
  Emotion Awareness Training

- **Behavioral Aspects**
  Self Management Training

- **Relational Aspects**
  Interpersonal/Social Skills Training
  Assertiveness Training
  Role Playing

- **Perceptual/Cognitive Aspects**
  Cognitive Awareness Training
  Problem Solving Skills
  Symptom Management Training
  Thought Stopping

5.6 Personality Disorders as Milder Forms of Major Psychiatric Disorders

A major area of research in psychobiology involves conceptualizing personality disorders as being on a continuum with Axis I disorders, which is called the **dimensional model**. A useful analogy is that of someone being heterozygous for a single gene disease — often called **Mendelian diseases** such as Huntington's disease or cystic fibrosis. Those who have a mixture of one affected and one non-affected gene may show an illness to a lesser extent (**forme fruste**) or not at all.

As described, major psychiatric disorders can be illustrated as disturbances in four key areas of function:

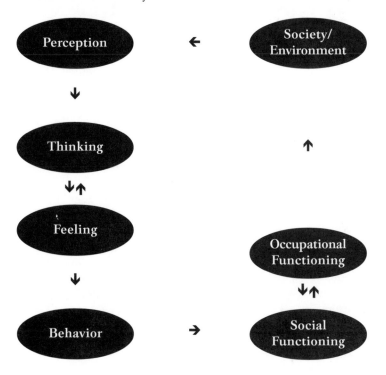

This scheme is helpful in conceptualizing the basic concept or major aberration in an illness. For example, schizophrenia can be considered primarily an illness of perception/cognition that is typically expressed by symptoms such as delusions, hallucinations and abnormal speech. However, there are also characteristic changes that occur in affective state (flattening of emotional responses) and behavior (disorganized or catatonic) that are key elements of this condition.

Combining the cognitive and perceptual aspects into one domain allows the derivation of the central concept for major psychiatric disorders:

Cognition/ Perception	Affective State	Behavior
Abnormal Findings	**Abnormal Findings**	**Abnormal Findings**

Abnormal Findings

Form of Thought
- Flight of ideas
- Loosening of assocations
- Derailment
- Blocking

Content of Thought
- Delusions
- Overvalued ideas

Perception
- Hallucinations
- Illusions
- Deperson-alization
- Derealization

Abnormal Findings

Affect is defined as the visible, external or objective manifestions of emotional state; it refers to the observation of momentary changes in emotions.

Mood refers to the subjective, internal emotional state; it is the pervasive tone displayed over time; it is described by the patient.

Abnormal Findings

There are many aberrations of behavior that are seen in Axis I disorders (e.g. tics, compulsions, catatonia, etc.).

A disorder of behavior can be considered an extreme along the continuum of being either too prone or too inhibited to act in everyday situations.

Axis I Conditions
- Schizophrenia
- Delusional Disorder

Axis I Conditions
- Mania (mood too high)
- Depression (mood too low)

Axis I Conditions
- Impulse-Control Disorders (deficit in behavioral inhibition)
- Anxiety Disorders (excess of behavioral inhibition)

If the degree of severity of the symptoms of Axis I conditions is lessened, there is an overlap with the core features of personality disorder clusters as follows:
- *Schizophrenia/Psychotic Disorders* — Cluster A: odd, eccentric, socially detached.

- *Mood Disorders/Impulse Control Disorders* — Cluster B: transient shifts in emotional state are more related to affect than mood; aggressive actions and impulsivity are characteristic of some of these disorders.
- *Anxiety Disorders* — Cluster C: avoidance of potentially aversive consequences; low tolerance for anxiety; overly restrained behavior.

5.7   The Mental Status Examination (MSE)

The previous section highlights the need to perform a mental status examination on all patients regardless of the diagnosis. The MSE is the part of the interview where cognitive functions are tested and inquiries are made about the symptoms of psychiatric conditions. It is a set of standardized observations and questions that evaluate perception, thinking, feeling, and behavior. The MSE records only the observed behavior, cognitive abilities and inner experiences expressed during the interview. A mnemonic for the MSE is as follows:

"ABC STAMP LICKER"*
Appearance
Behavior
Cooperation

Speech
Thought — **form** and **content**
Affect — visible moment-to-moment variation in emotion
Mood — subjective emotional tone throughout the interview
Perception — in all sensory modalities

Level of consciousness
Insight & Judgment
Cognitive functioning & Sensorium
    Orientation
    Memory
    Attention & Concentration
    Reading & Writing
Knowledge base
Endings — suicidal and/or homicidal ideation
Reliability of the information supplied

5.8   A Rationale for the Use of Psychotropic Medication

Based on the presentation up to this point, there are three main aspects of personality disorders that provide the basis for using psychotropic medication:
- The dimensional model with Axis I disorders
- Alteration of genetic/temperamental factors
- Concomitant Axis I & Axis II disorders

The Dimensional Model

The dimensional model discussed earlier in this chapter extends to more than a theoretical association between the personality disorder clusters and the corresponding Axis I disorders previously listed. Siever (1991) listed a number of physical findings (biological indices) found in both major psychiatric and personality disorders:

- Eye movement (tracking) abnormalities
- Impaired task performance
- Neurotransmitter abnormalities
- Anatomic changes
- Brain electrical abnormalities

- Impaired task performance
- Neurotransmitter response to stimulation
- Electrical changes in skin conductivity

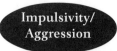

- Sleep architecture changes
- Neurotransmitter response to stimulation

- Aautonomic response (heart rate)
- Orienting responses
- Physical response to stimulation

Not all of the above biological findings are present in patients with either major psychiatric or personality disorders, but there is enough of an overlap to give credence to the dimensional model. Given that there are effective pharmacologic treatments for many of the Axis I conditions, an argument can be made to treat the shared, underlying biological/genetic mechanisms with the same medications. Another view based on the dimensional model considers symptoms common to both Axis I and Axis II conditions. **Symptom-focused treatment** extracts component symptoms from the patient's presenting complaints. These personality symptoms are then treated pharmacologically according to the recommended management if they were part of a major psychiatric disorder. For example:

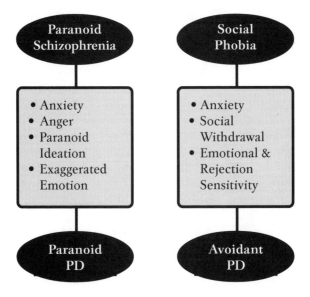

Each of the features common to these disorders is amenable to treatment (to a greater or lesser extent) with medication. This approach seeks to extract for pharmacotherapeutic treatment symptoms related to genetic, structural or neurochemical changes (in essence, the biological from biopsychosocial amalgamation). Features such as disturbances in interpersonal relationships, limited insight and poor judgment are not treatable by medication. A partial list of symptoms which are amenable to pharmacologic interventions is as follows:

Symptom	Medication Category
• Anhedonia/dysphoria	Antidepressants
• Anxiety	Anxiolytics
• Impulsivity/ADHD	Mood stabilizers, Stimulants
• Insomnia	Sedative/hypnotics
• Mood swings	Mood stabilizers, Antidepressants
• Perceptual disturbances	Antipsychotics
• Substance abuse	naltrexone, disulfiram

Genetic/Temperamental Factors

The initial three temperamental factors presented in Cloninger (1987) can be related to the action of a key neurotransmitter:

Reward Dependence	Harm Avoidance	Novelty Seeking
Principal Neurotransmitter **Dopamine**	Principal Neurotransmitter **Serotonin**	Principal Neurotransmitter **Norepinephrine**

Dopaminergic tracts in the brain receive input from several areas and then project to the forebrain where they are involved in behavioral activation.

Dopamine release is enhanced by amphetamine and cocaine use, and is considered an integral part of the brain's reward system.

Serotonergic tracts are mainly in the rostral and caudal raphe nuclei. They project to three main areas in brain:
• Basal ganglia (movement)
• Limbic system (emotion)
• Cerebral cortex (cognition and many other functions)

Serotonin has been linked to violent and suicidal behavior.

Noradrenergic cells arise from the locus ceruleus and project to the hypothalamus and limbic system. Norepinephrine is thought to be a key factor in learning and some memory functions. In this capacity, it prevents the forgetting of behaviors that were previously rewarded. It has many connections to serotonergic neurons.

While this presentation is overly reductionistic, it is useful in linking some of the key neurotransmitters involved in psychiatric disorders to genetically-based behavior. Cloninger (1987) provides a more elegant explanation of this association, as do Bates & Wachs (1994).

Co-Existing Axis I & Axis II Disorders

Personality-disordered patients are more likely to develop Axis I disorders than the general population. Mood, anxiety and substance-related disorders are common **comorbid** conditions. Major psychiatric disorders complicate the treatment of personality disorders and vice versa. Ascribing symptoms to one particular condition can be difficult because they often arise from similar vulnerabilities and processes. Age of onset, chronicity and severity are generally not helpful in distinguishing personality disorders from major psychiatric conditions.

A personality disorder, which may well be the priority for treatment, is often overlooked when an Axis I disorder coexists. Assigning a separate axis for personality disorders, which started with the DSM-III, helped highlight the need to consider these conditions.

Axis I and II disorders can have a reciprocal effect on each other. For example, a patient with a dependent personality disorder can foreseeably develop a major depressive episode when a relationship ends. Conversely, a lifetime of suffering from a condition such as agoraphobia could quite reasonably be seen as causing aberrations in personality development that would fall into the dependent realm.

In general, a coexisting personality disorder has the following effects on major mental illnesses:
- Earlier age of onset
- Worsening of the course (including suicide attempts)
- Respond less completely and less predictably to treatment
- Higher rate of recurrence/relapse of the illness
- Lowered compliance with treatment for either condition
- The personality disorder often improves with treatment of the Axis I disorder

The symptoms of a personality disorder may need to be addressed first if they interfere with the treatment of other conditions. For example, the socially-controlling behavior exhibited in narcissistic personality disorder can negatively influence participation in group therapy for substance abuse. In some illnesses (e.g. schizophrenia), some personality disorders are excluded from consideration because the effect of the illness is so severe that aberrant personality formation is presumed to occur virtually automatically. Hogg (1990) investigated the prevalence of personality disorders at the onset of schizophrenia and found that over half of the patients had personality disorders, the most common being schizotypal (21%), and then borderline and antisocial (15% each). Substance use disorders present a "chicken or egg" argument about cause and effect. Vaillant (1983) asserted that maladaptive interpersonal characteristics arise from alcoholism, while others have argued the converse. Patients with alcohol abuse are much more likely to have an antisocial or borderline personality disorder (BPD), which often affects recovery. For example, in non-personality disordered patients, a socially positive milieu promotes the likelihood of relapse while in patients with BPD, a negative social interaction is more likely to cause the resumption of consumption.

5.9   Selection of Medication

The following two brief cases will be used to illustrate the delineation of target symptoms for treatment with medication:

Case 1

A forty-year old female news reporter has been paired with the same male camera operator for several years. Although their contact was exclusively work related, she felt a growing closeness and hoped that a relationship would start, aided by the fact that they had been unattached to others for this interval. When he announced that he his engagement to another woman, she accused him of leading her on and wasting her most "eligible" years. She threw her microphone at him and complained to the station manager that the quality of his work had deteriorated to the point she could no longer work with him.

Case 2

Norman is a fifty-year old male systems administrator who works for a company with offices across the nation. While the caliber of his work was satisfactory, he had both sought transfers to other regions and had this suggested by his supervisors. This had happened so often than his reputation usually preceded him. Upon starting at yet another new office, some mischievous co-workers altered the lettering on his cubicle to the name "Nomad," which upset him greatly. He became vigilant for other practical jokes and refused to join his colleagues for lunch so he wouldn't have to leave his desk unattended.

The following target symptoms can be extracted from these histories:

	Psychosocial	Temperamental
Case 1	limited insight poor judgment	affective instability impulsivity
Case 2	interpersonal difficulties rejection sensitivity	suspiciousness social withdrawal

Dividing presenting symptoms into psychosocial/character and biological/temperamental characteristics helps focus treatment interventions. There are a small but growing number of studies showing that patients with personality disorders have different neuroendocrine responses than controls (Siever, 1992; Steinberg, 1994) and on this basis may warrant a trial of medication in addition to psychotherapy and skills training to address the temperament dimension. Expanding on the work of Siever & Davis (1991), the selection of medications can be made according the following scheme:

Dimension of Pathology	Personality Cluster	Associated Neurotransmitter	Category of Medication
Cognitive-Perceptual	A	Dopamine	Antipsychotics
Impulsivity-Aggression	B (ASPD, BPD)	Serotonin	Selective Serotonin Reuptake Inhibitors (SSRIs)
Affective Instability	B	Cholinergic/ Noradrenergic	Tricyclic Anti-depressants (TCAs); Monoamine Oxidase Inhibitors (MAOIs)
Anxiety-Inhibition	C	Biogenic Amines	Benzo-diazepines SSRIs, MAOIs

• **Neuroleptics**, also called **antipsychotic medications**, are principally used for the acute and prophylactic treatment of psychotic disorders. There are over ten different classes of these medications, however a popular distinction is made between traditional and novel agents based on their mode of action. Traditional agents block the action of dopamine at dopamine type 2 (D_2) receptors. Novel or atypical agents are also referred to as serotonin-dopamine antagonists and agent has a unique profile of receptor subtype affinities.

• **Mood stabilizers** consist of lithium and anticonvulsant medications. The newer antipsychotic medications are also receiving indications for mood disorders as well. The principal indications for these agents are the acute and chronic treatment of mood disorders, however there are a considerable (and growing) number of other indications for these medications. In particular, these agents are used in bipolar disorders but have been found to be helpful in unipolar (major) depression. Not all anticonvulsants have uses in psychiatric disorders — the two currently in greatest use are carbamazepine and valproate (divalproex).

• **Antidepressant** medications also encompass a wide range of different chemical categories and have a considerable number of uses beyond treating depression. Tricyclic antidepressants (TCAs) and monoamine oxidase inhibitors (MAOIs) were the first two categories. Newer antidepressants had modifications to the tricyclic structure and are known as heterocyclic antidepressants (HCAs). Selective serotonin reuptake inhibitors (SSRIs) and newer agents (called atypical) have been increasingly used in the treatment of personality disorders.

• **Sedative/hypnotics** are also called anxiolytics and sleeping pills, respectively. The anti-anxiety agents are dominated by the group called benzodiazepines, of which the most common agent is diazepam (Valium®). Other medications besides the benzodiazepines have shown to be helpful in diminishing anxiety. Some benzodiazepines are also indicated for treating insomnia, in addition to other medications that have less chance of causing dependence (habituation).

• Other medications have been used in treating personality disorders such as stimulants, anticholinergic agents and opiate antagonists. Many case reports have been published advocating the use of certain agents and combinations of medications.

Medication Infobits

• One of the many intriguing aspects of psychopharmacology is the multitude of uses not only for categories of medications, but for individual agents. For example, aside from mood disorders, antidepressants are useful in chronic pain, sexual dysfunction, premenstrual syndrome, organic syndromes (pseudobulbar affect), eating disorders and for enuresis, sleepwalking and night terrors in children. Lithium is useful as a mood stabilizer, antidepressant and augmenting agent, as well as being used to decrease aggression and cluster headaches.

• Where possible, avoid medications which have a high potential for lethality in overdose or addiction, or become dangerous in combination or with substances of abuse. The TCAs are the most worrisome because they cause cardiac rhythm disturbances.

• As the severity of the personality disorder increases, higher doses or combinations of medications may be required

5.10 Limitations in the Use of Medication

Overall, there remains a paucity of methodologically sound studies showing the clear efficacy of medications in the treatment of personality disorders. In summary, no specific pharmacologic intervention has been consistently shown to be effective for a specific personality disorder or a particular constellation of symptoms. Borderline personality disorder has been the focus of the majority of reports, with the schizotypal personality disorder being the second most studied condition, due to its presumed genetic association to schizophrenia.

The relative lack of controlled studies in and of itself is not a reason to avoid using medication. Studies showing unequivocal support for many types of psychotherapy are still awaited, as is a clear rationale for choosing a particular type of psychotherapy for an individual patient. A considerable clinical lore (anecdotes and case reports) has developed regarding the response of individual patients. A this point in time, there is no reliable way of knowing which patients will predictably respond to particular medications. A significant placebo effect is operative in the treatment of personality disorders.

Published reports, studies and texts contain a wide range of avidity for the use of medications in Axis II conditions. Many caution against the widespread use of pharmacologic agents, and none advocate using medication without some form of concurrent psychotherapy.

The rationale for using medications in the treatment of personality disorders is based on two main areas of research:

- The dimensional model, where personality disorders are considered to be on a continuum with Axis I disorders (which have well-established pharmacologic treatments); the more closely the symptoms of a personality disorder resembles an Axis I condition, the more likely is the response to medication

- Relating specific psychopathology to the action of specific neurotransmitters, as in the work of Cloninger (1987) and Siever & Davis (1991); in this view, symptoms are not grouped into DSM-IV-TR diagnoses, but instead according to which neurotransmitter is putatively linked to the dysfunctional behavior. In other words, rather than saying, "antidepressants are useful for patients with borderline personality disorder," this approach would be instead be expressed by a statement such as "patients with reduced impulse-control may benefit from a trial of a mood stabilizer."

5.11 What About "Chemical Imbalances?"
The term "chemical imbalance" has become a popular explanation for many mental and emotional disorders. While perceptions, cognitions, emotions and behaviors are chemically mediated by neurotransmitters, the term lacks specificity and does little to indicate the source of the imbalance. While "genetics" or "stress" are common explanations for the onset of chemical imbalances, this places too little emphasis on elucidating psychosocial precipitants, and does not foster introspection or the development of insight. Keeping a biopsychosocial perspective with patients keeps a balance and avoids the notion that there are simple explanations and quick fixes.

5.12 Special Considerations
Timing and Introduction of Medication
It is generally advisable to discuss the possibility of using medication at the outset of treatment. Patients can be told that certain symptoms may be more amenable to medical treatment, may be treated faster pharmacologically, and that complications can arise during psychotherapy (e.g. concurrent depression) that will require medication.

It is important to avoid the perception that medication is being given as a last resort, which both the therapist and patient can contribute to independently. The successful use of medication is influenced by the therapist's confidence in these agents and the way they are introduced in to treatment. If a referral for medication is made because of an impasse in therapy, pessimism about the efficacy can come from the therapist and the prescriber. Similarly, at times of crisis, considerable pressure can be put on prescribers to "do something." Because medications can be switched, increased or decreased quickly, this often becomes the desired (or at least easiest) intervention. Because most crises are interpersonal in nature, adjusting medication is unlikely to be effective and can deleteriously affect treatment. Wherever possible, it is best to define specific symptoms or symptom complexes as the target of medication and not deviate from this when interpersonal storms arise.

It also important to explain the role and limitations of medications. For example, many agents have a delayed onset of action, have predictable side effects and be substituted with another agent if the person doesn't respond. Silk (1996) provides a comprehensive guide to the use of medications in patients with personality disorders.

Medication as an Entity

In general, patients with personality disorders can be seen as being fixed at a less-developed level of functioning. Akin to children using teddy bears as a symbolic reminder of their parents (**transitional objects**), patients can come to view the pill or tablet as a symbolic reminder of the therapist. Patients may seek medication in order to receive a tangible item and/or something that will remind them of the therapist between sessions.

Patients may begin to speak about their medication as an entity separate from the prescriber, and assign to it good or bad qualities (e.g. it helped them, caused troubling side effects, etc). The pill or tablet can be seen an ally that is always there for the patient day and night. A strong attachment can develop towards a certain medications or dosages, and for this reason considerable resistance can develop to stopping the prescription even when there is little biochemical benefit in continuing the medication.

Separate Providers

In situations where the therapist is not a medical doctor or has prescribing privileges, the medication will need to be provided by someone else, usually a psychiatrist or family doctor. Even among psychiatrists, many choose to treat patients with either psychotherapy or pharmacotherapy and refer patients elsewhere for the other type of treatment. This sets up a four-way interaction, with each dimension having its own transferences:

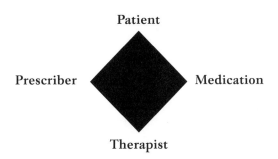

In such instances, mutual respect for each other's abilities and communication between the two parties is essential. For example, a psychotherapist may see pharmacotherapy as a blunt instrument with which to treat patients, while a biologically-oriented psychiatrist may see psychotherapy as an inefficient means of treatment. Having a working knowledge of each field and being appraised of the limitations of each specialty helps keep these disparate forms of treatment in perspective. Ultimately, the goal is the well being of the patient, which is assisted by respecting professional differences.

In some cases, treatment with medication promotes a faster resolution of symptoms than by psychotherapy. This situation can create a special challenge. The patient may feel symptomatically better, for example, after a few doses of anxiolytic medication or a few weeks of taking an antidepressant and not wish to return to psychotherapy. Even short-term, structured therapies last at least several weeks and may cause a period of initial worsening as patients are faced with the effects of their actions and become increasingly aware of the maladaptive nature of their interpersonal styles.

On the other hand, a patient who suffers severe side-effects may develop a bias against ever using psychiatric medications again. In these situations, it is most helpful if gains and setbacks are best not immediately ascribed to one particular person or intervention. Lasting gains in treatment are slow and almost always accompanied by setbacks. Complicating this is the notion of a "cure" and the goals of treatment. A complete personality make-over is not realistic. Instead, goals that are attainable are more along the lines of:
- Fostering an awareness of dysfunctional patterns
- Increasing adaptive behaviors (improving judgment)
- Promoting more effective coping strategies and relationships (changing behavior)
- Double checking one's perception of events
- Decreasing symptoms

Some patients, particularly those who externalize the locus of their difficulties may well feel that the medication has "accomplished everything" and not wish to participate in a fuller treatment program despite the urging of everyone else involved. A detailed discussion of the negotiating the therapist-prescriber split is provided in Koenigsberg (1993) and Woodward (1993).

5.13 References

Bates JE & Wachs TD
Temperament: Individual Differences at the Interface of Biology & Behavior
American Psychological Association, Washington DC, 1994

Chess S & A. Thomas A
Temperament in Clinical Practice
The Guilford Press, New York, 1986

Cloninger CR
A systematic method for clinical description and classification of personality variants.
Archives of General Psychiatry 44: p. 573-588, 1987

Cloninger CR, Svrakic DM & Przybeck TR
A psychobiological model of temperament and character.
Archives of General Psychiatry 50: p. 975-990, 1993

Costa PT & McCrae RR
Four ways five factors are basic.
Pers Individual Diff, 13: p. 652-665, 1992

Costello C, Editor
Personality Characteristics of the Personality Disordered
Wiley & Sons, New York, 1996

Gray JA
The Neuropsychology of Anxiety
Oxford University Press, New York, 1982

Engel GL
The concept of psychosomatic disorder
J Psychosom Res 11: p. 3-9, 1967

Engel GL
The need for a new medical model: a challenge for biomedicine
Science 196: p. 129-136, 1977

Freeman A & Davison M
Short-Term Therapy for the Long-Term Patient, in
Innovations in Clinical Practice, Volume 15
Vandecreek L, Knappy S & Jackson T, Editors
Professional Resource Press, Sarasota, FL, 1997

Hogg B, Jackson HJ, Rudd RP et al.
Diagnosing personality disorders in recent-onset schizophrenia.
J Nerv Ment. Dis. 178: p. 194-199, 1990

Joseph S
Personality Disorders: New Symptom-Focused Drug Therapy
The Haworth Medical Press, New York, 1997

Kagan J, Resnick JS, Snidman N, Gibbons J & Johnson MO
Childhood derivatives of inhibition and lack of inhibition to the unfamiliar.
Child Dev 59: p. 1580-1589, 1988

Koenigsberg HW, in
American Psychiatric Press Review of Psychiatry, Volume 12
J. M. Oldham, M. B. Riba & A. Tasman, Editors
American Psychiatric Press, Inc., Washington DC, 1993

Lipowski ZJ
What does the word "psychosomatic" really mean?
Psychosomatic Medicine 46: p. 153-171, 1984

Loehlin JC
Are personality traits differentially heritable?
Behav Genet 12: p. 417 - 428, 1982

Siever LJ & Davis KL
A psychobiological perspective on personality disorders.
American Journal of Psychiatry 148(12): p. 1647-1658, 1991

Siever LJ, Corcarro EF & Trestman RL
The growth hormone response to clonidine in acute and remitted depressed male patients.
Neuropsychopharmacology 6: p. 165-177, 1992

Silk KR, in
Clinical Assessment and Management of Severe Personality Disorders
Links PS, Editor
American Psychiatric Press, Inc., Washington, DC, 1996

Sigvardsson S, Bohman M & Cloninger CR
Structure and stability of childhood personality: prediction of later social adjustment.
J Child Psychol Psychiatry 28: p. 929-946, 1987

Sperry L
Cognitive Behavior Therapy of DSM-IV Personality Disorders
Brunner/Mazel, New York, 1999

Steinberg BJ, Trestman RL & Siever LJ, in
Biological and Neurobehavioral Studies of Borderline Personality Disorder
Silk KR, Editor
American Psychiatric Press, Inc. Washington DC, 1994

Svrakic DM, Whitehead C, Przybeck TR & Cloninger CR
Differential diagnosis of personality disorders by the seven-factor model of temperament and character.
Archives of General Psychiatry 50: p. 991-999, 1993

Tellengen A, in
Anxiety and the Anxiety Disorders
Tuma AH & Maser J, Editors
Lawrence Erlbaum Associates, Hillsdale, NJ, 1985

Woodward B, Duckworth KS & Gutheil TG, in
American Psychiatric Press Review of Psychiatry, Volume 12
Oldham JM, Riba MB & Tasman A, Editors
American Psychiatric Press, Inc. Washington DC, 1993

Vaillant GE
The Natural History of Alcoholism: Causes, Patterns and Paths to Recovery
Harvard University Press, Cambridge, MA, 1983

Chapter 6

Psychological Testing & Diagnostic Interviews

6.1 How Can Psychological Testing Help to Make a Diagnosis?

The use of **psychological testing**, also called **psychometric testing**, provides a method for personality assessment beyond the criteria set out in the DSM-IV-TR or ICD-lO. Testing yields valuable diagnostic information and can be used to monitor progress or prognosis. Most commonly used instruments have a standard protocol for administration and scoring. This helps ensure the critical issues of reliability (the test gives consistent results) and validity (the test measures what it is supposed to measure).

Inherent in the scoring is a concept of normality. Since the tables used in these tests were assembled empirically, relatively "normal" people were tested to provide the standardized data. Different concepts of normality exist. The model used in statistics is the bell-shaped curve, where some measure of behavior is plotted numerically with deviation seen at the extreme ends. While this lends itself nicely to numerical interpretations, it is somewhat artificial in that aspects of a personality or behavior cannot always be translated into a scoring system.

Many definitions of normality exist; with common themes being:
• Strength of character
• Flexibility/ability to adjust
• Ability to learn from experience
• Ability to laugh and experience pleasure without conflict
• Ability to work
• Ability to love another person
• Ability to achieve insight
• Degree of acculturation

Psychological tests for personality disorders fall into two main categories. **Projective tests** have an ambiguous content requiring the examinees to "project" something of themselves into their answers, which are neither wrong nor right and are not scored numerically. Projected answers reveal the needs, conflicts, wishes, perceptions and defenses of those taking the test. Interpretation is based on different theories of personality development. **Objective tests** are highly structured with specific questions yielding numerical results derived from standardized scoring schemes.

6.2 Projective Assessments

Forer Structured Sentence Completion Test (FSSCT)

Author: Forer BR, 1957

Synopsis
- Consists of 100 partial sentences developed to identify individuals' attitudes and views about themselves, others, and the world
- The structure of the FSSCT involves both the specificity of the partial sentences and the evaluation system used to assess the quality of responses
- Evaluation forms contain a structured evaluation scheme that the examiner then uses to group individual items into one of four categories: Interpersonal Figures, Wishes, Causes of Own (feelings and behaviors), and Reactions (to other people)
- Each item is rated according to "attitudes toward" and "characteristics of" in the first two categories and "attitudes toward" in the last two categories
- All terms used in the FSSCT have specific definitions and clear implications about the structure and organization of one's personality – these are outlined in the user's manual

Source
Western Psychological Services
12031 Wilshire Blvd.
Los Angeles, CA   90025-1251
Telephone: 1-800-648-8857 (U.S. and Canada), 1-310-478-2061
Fax: 1-310-478-7838
Web Address: http://www.wpspublish.com/Inetpub4/index.htm

Holtzman Inkblot Test (HIT)

Author: Holtzman WH, 1961

Synopsis
- Designed to overcome some of the deficiencies of the Rorschach
- Unlike the Rorschach, the HIT is a standardized measurement with clearly defined, objective scoring criteria
- Examiner shows each of the 47 cards (45 test cards, 2 practice cards) one at a time to the subject asks what he sees in the inkblot
- Only one response per inkblot is requested; the examiner may ask subject to clarify or elaborate on a response
- HIT is then scored against 22 variables (reaction time, rejection, location, space, form definiteness, form appropriateness, color, shading, movement, pathognomonic verbalization, integration, content (human, animal, anatomy, sex, abstract), anxiety, hostility, barrier, penetration, balance, and popular)

Source
The Psychological Corporation
c/o Harcourt Assessment, Inc.
19500 Bulverde Rd.
San Antonio, TX 78259
Telephone: 1-800-211-8378
Fax: 1-800-232-1223
Web Address: http://harcourtassessment.com

Rorschach Ink Blots

Author: Rorschach H, 1921

Synopsis
- Consists of 10 cards (5 color, 5 black & white)
- Subject is asked to describe what he sees on the cards
- Responses are scored according to
  (i) the location in the blot of what is seen by the subject
  (ii) the kind of characteristic emphasized (e.g., form or color)
  (iii) the content of what is seen (e.g., animal)
- Subject's response scored compared to established norms
- Interpretation is not highly standardized
- Test has been criticized as being unreliable, even in the areas of diagnosis and prognosis in which it is most frequently used

Source
Hogrefe & Huber Publishers
875 Massachusetts Avenue, 7th Floor
Cambridge, MA   02139
Telephone: 1-866-823-4726   Fax: 1-617-354-6875
Web address: www.hhpub.com

Rotter Incomplete Sentences Blank (RISB), 2nd Ed.

Authors: Rotter JM, Rah MI & Raferty JE, 1992

Synopsis
- Used as a screening of overall adjustment
- Consists of 40 unfinished sentences that the subject is required to complete (e.g., "If only I could......")
- Responses are scored on a 6-point scale (with 3 being neutral)
- Responses are categorized as either positive (an optimistic frame of mind) or conflicting (indicating hostility and pessimism)

Source
The Psychological Corporation (see p. 118)

Thematic Apperception Test

Author: Murray H, 1973

Synopsis
- Among the most widely used, researched, and taught projective tests
- Consists of a series of pictures of ambiguous scenes to which subjects are requested to make up stories or fantasies concerning what is, has, and is going to happen, along with a description of the thoughts and feelings of the various characters depicted
- Test provides examiner with a rich source of data, based on the subject's perceptions and imagination for use in the understanding of the subject's current needs, motives, emotions, and conflicts, both conscious and unconscious
- Use in clinical assessment is generally part of a larger battery of tests and interview data

Source
The Psychological Corporation (see p. 118)

6.3   Objective/Structured Assessments

Borderline Personality Organization Scale (BPO)

Authors: Oldham J, Clarkin J, Appelbaum A, Carr A, Kernberg P, Lotterman A & Haas G, 1985

Synopsis
• Developed through a factor analysis of a 130-item questionnaire designed by the authors
• 30-item scale with the strongest factor loadings for each of three sub-scales: identity diffusion, primitive defenses, and reality testing
• The BPO scale has been shown to be correlated with frequency and severity of violence in abusive men

Source
American Psychiatric Publishing, Inc.
1000 Wilson Boulevard, Suite 1825
 Arlington, VA   22209-3901
Telephone: 703-907-7322 or 800-368-5777
Fax: 703-907-1091
Web Address: www.appi.org

Coolidge Assessment Battery (CAB)

Author: Coolidge FL, 1999

Synopsis
- Provides a comprehensive assessment of all DSM-IV-TR Personality Disorders and five major Axis I disorders
- Consists of 225 items with a total of 56 scales, including:
  - 7 Axis I scales including depression, anxiety, schizophrenia, PTSD and social phobia
  - 12 Axis II scales which closely follow DSM-IV diagnostic criteria
  - Neuropsychological dysfunction scales including memory, language, and executive functions (including decision making, planning and task completion)
  - Hostility scales for anger, dangerousness and impulsivity
  - Scales for assessment of overall maladjustment: withdrawal, frustration tolerance and depersonalization
- Items are rated on a 4-point rating scale: Strongly False, More False than True, More True than False and Strongly True; this makes the CAB more sensitive than inventories which use only true/false response sets

Source
Sigma Assessment Systems, Inc.
511 Fort Street, Suite 435
P.O. Box 610984
Port Huron, MI 48061-0984
Telephone: 1-800-265-1285
Fax: 1-800-361-9411
Web Address: www.sigmaassessmentsystems.com

Diagnostic Interview for Borderlines, Revised (DIB-R)

Authors: Zanarini MC, Gunderson JG, Franckenburg FR & Chauncey DL, 1989

Synopsis
- Developed specifically to assess for borderline personality disorder
- Based on DSM-IV criteria
- Assesses symptoms in 4 primary areas:
    (i)   Affect (e.g. hopelessness, worthlessness, guilt, anger, anxiety, etc.)
    (ii) Cognition (e.g., odd thinking, unusual perceptions, non-delusional paranoia, quasi-psychosis)
    (iii) Impulse Action Patterns (e.g., substance abuse/dependence, sexual deviance, manipulative suicide gestures)
    (iv) Interpersonal Relationships (e.g., intolerance of aloneness, abandonment/engulfment/annihilation fears, counterdependency, stormy relationships)

Source
Mary C. Zanarini
c/o McLean Hospital
115 Mill St.
Belmont, MA 02178-9106
Telephone: 1-617-855-2293
Fax: 1-617-855-3522

Dimensional Assessment of Personality Pathology – Basic Questionnaire (DAPP-BQ)

Authors: Livesley WJ & Jackson DN (2004 – in press)

Synopsis
- A 290-item self-report measure
- Assesses 18 traits to provide a representation of the overall domain of personality disorders
- Traits include affective lability, anxiousness, callousness, cognitive dysregulation, compulsivity, conduct problems, identity problems, insecure attachment, intimacy problems, narcissism, oppositionality, rejection, restricted expression, self-harm, social avoidance, stimulus seeking, submissiveness, and suspiciousness

Source
Research Psychologists Press
P.O. Box 3292, Station B
London, ON, Canada   N6A 4K3
Telephone:1-800-401-4480
Fax: 1-800-361-9411
Web Address: www.rpp.on.ca

Eysenck Personality Questionnaire – Revised (EPQ-R)

Authors: Eysenck HJ & Eysenck SBG, 1993

Synopsis
- 106 items (a 48-item version is also available)
- Used for clinical diagnosis, occupational counseling, personnel selection/placement
- Measures on 4 different scales: Tough-mindedness, Introversion/Extraversion, Emotionality, and a Lie Scale
- Measures 3 main personality factors: psychoticism, extraversion, and neuroticism

Source
Hodder & Stoughton Educational
c/o Hodder Headline PLC
338 Euston Road
London NW1 3BH   England
Telephone: 0207 873 6000
Fax: 0207 873 6024
Web address: www.hoddertests.co.uk

International Personality Disorder Examination (IPDE)

Author: Loranger AW, 1995

Synopsis
- Used to identify traits/behaviors relevant to an assessment of the criteria for diagnosis of personality disorders
- Composed of 2 modules:
  — IPDE DSM-IV, which closely resembles the Personality Disorder Examination (PDE) with minor differences (the PDE is based on DSM-III-R criteria)
  — IPDE ICD-10, which is separate and consists of the diagnostic criteria for personality disorders according to the ICD-10
- Both modules are very similar and often contain identical questions, however, rating criteria for each are different
- The most widely established measure of personality disorders currently available

Source
Psychological Assessment Resources, Inc.
16204 N. Florida Avenue
Lutz, FL   33549-8119
Phone: 1-800-331-TEST (8378) (U.S. & Canada)
Fax: 1-800-727-9329
Web Address: www.parinc.com

Millon Clinical Multiaxial Inventory
3rd Edition (MCMI-III)

Authors: Millon T, Davis R & Millon C, 1997

Synopsis
- An update of the MCMI-II representing ongoing research, conceptual developments, and changes in the DSM-IV
- Assesses a wide range of information related to personality, emotionality, and test-taking attitude
- Consists of 175 items/28 clinical personality scales:
- Modifying Indices (Disclosure, Desirability, Debasement, Validity), Clinical Personality Patterns (Schizoid, Avoidant, Depressive, Dependent, Histrionic, Narcissistic, Antisocial, Aggressive (Sadistic), Compulsive, Passive-Aggressive (Negativistic), Self-Defeating), Severe Personality Pathology (Schizotypal, Borderline, Paranoid), Clinical Syndromes (Anxiety, Somatoform, Bipolar, Manic, Dysthymia, Alcohol Dependence, Drug Dependence, Post-Traumatic Stress Disorder), Severe Clinical Syndromes (Thought Disorder, Major Depression, Delusional Disorder)
- Brief in comparison to other personality inventories, has a strong theoretical basis, administration and scoring are simple

Source
Pearson Assessments
1313 Lone Oak Rd
Eagan, MN 55121-1334
Telephone: 1-800-627-7271, ext. 3225 or 1-952-681-3225
Fax: 1-800-632-9011 or 1-952-681-3299
Web address: www.pearsonassessments.com

Minnesota Multiphasic Personality Inventory-II (MMPI-II)

Authors: Hathaway S & McKinley JC, 1989

Synopsis
• An objective personality test for assessment of psychopathology, designed to assess major patterns of personality, emotional, and behavioral disorders
• Consists of 567 statements that the subject marks as being true or false
• Internal checks are in place within the assessment that can determine if the general requirements have not been satisfied
• 8 clinical scales: Scale 1 (Hypochondriasis); Scale 2 (Depression); Scale 3 (Hysteria); Scale 4 (Psychopathic Deviate); Scale 6 (Paranoia); Scale 7 (Psychasthenia); Scale 8 (Schizophrenia); and Scale 9 (Hypomania)
• 2 scales added from within the original MMPI: Scale 5 (Masculinity-Femininity) and Scale 0 (Social Introversion)
• 3 scales designed to estimate the validity of the clinical profile:
• L (Lie) Scale (has statements dealing with a common, relatively insignificant weakness to which most people are willing to confess);
• F (Infrequency) Scale (made up of statements that were answered in the keyed direction by less than 10% of the inventory's original standardization group);
• K Scale (designed to trap the respondent who attempts to conceal actual psychopathology)

Source
Pearson Assessments (see p. 127)

NEO Five-Factor Inventory (NEO-FFI)

Authors: Costa PT & McCrae RR, 1989/1992

Synopsis
- designed to assess the personality domains as outlined by the Five Factor Model (FFM): Neuroticism, Extraversion, Conscientiousness, Openness to Experience, and Agreeableness
- Consists of 60 items, rated on a 5-point scale (a shortened version of the 240-item NEO Personality Inventory-Revised (NEO PI-R))

Source
Psychological Assessment Resources, Inc. (see p. 126)

NEO Personality Inventory – Revised (NEO-PI-R)

Authors: Costa PT & McCrae RR, 1992

Synopsis
- Contains 2 forms: Form S – Self Report, Form R – Observer Report
- Each form consists of 240 items, plus 3 validity items
- Designed to assess the personality domains as outlined by the Five-Factor Model: Neuroticism, Extraversion, Conscientiousness, Openness to Experience, and Agreeableness
- Includes the 6 traits that define each domain

Source
Psychological Assessment Resources, Inc. (see p. 126)

OMNI-IV Personality Disorder Inventory

Author: Loranger AW, 1997

Synopsis
• A comprehensive self-report measure of abnormal personality traits
• Consists of 210 items, 10 personality disorder scales (based on DSM-IV criteria for personality disorders)
• Includes a "Current Distress" scale to assess the subject's mental state during the week prior to the test date

Source
Psychological Assessment Resources, Inc. (see p. 126)

Personality Assessment Inventory® (PAI®)

Author: Morey LC, 1991

Synopsis
• Designed to provide information relevant to clinical diagnosis, treatment planning, and screening for psychopathology
• Self-report inventory of adult psychopathology designed as a multi-dimensional alternative to the Minnesota Multiphasic Personality Inventory (MMPI) for assessing abnormal personality traits
• Consists of 344 items (scored on a 4-point ordinal scale: F = False; ST = Slightly True; MT = Mainly True; VT = Very True)
• Scales measured: Inconsistency, Infrequency, Negative Impression, Positive Impression, Somatic Complaints, Anxiety, Anxiety- Related Disorders, Depression, Mania, Paranoia, Schizophrenia, Borderline Features, Antisocial Features, Alcohol Problems, Drug Problems, Aggression, Suicidal Ideation, Stress, Nonsupport, Treatment Rejection, Dominance, Warmth.

Source
The Psychological Corporation (see p. 118)

Personality Assessment Schedule (PAS)

Author: Tyrer P, 1988

Synopsis
- One of the earliest semi-structured interviews
- Includes 24 personality characteristics rated on a 9-point scale
- Based on the ICD classification system
- Personality disorders assessed includes: explosive, paranoid-aggressive, anankastic, asthenic, schizoid, and histrionic
- Involves interviewing both the subject and a close informant; subject's responses are more heavily weighted in the final score

Source
Department of Public Mental Health
London W2 1PD United Kingdom
Telephone: 0207-886-1648
Fax: 0207-886-1995

Personality Diagnostic Questionnaire 4th Edition (PDQ-4)

Authors: Hyler SE, Oldham JM, Kellman HD & Doidge N, 1992

Synopsis
- Consists of 100 true/false questions for diagnoses of Axis II personality disorders in accordance with DSM-IV criteria
- Personality disorders assessed include schizoid, schizotypal, depressive-histrionic, narcissistic, borderline/antisocial/conduct disorder, avoidant, dependent, obsessive-compulsive negativistic and depressive
- Criticized a high number of false positive results; the latest version includes a Clinical Significance Scale to address this issue

Source
Telephone: 1-800-424-9537
Web Address: http://www.pdq4.com/#head_8

Personality Disorder Interview (PDI-IV)

Authors: Widiger TA, Mangine S, Corbitt EM, Ellis CG & Thomas GV, 1995

Synopsis
• Consists of 317 questions assessing each of 94 diagnostic criteria for 10 established and 2 proposed personality disorders (according to the DSM-IV)
• Divided into 2 formats: thematic and disorder
  — Thematic format consists of 9 themes: attitudes toward self, attitude toward others, security or comfort with others, friendships and relationships, conflicts and disagreements, work and leisure, social norms, mood, and appearance and perception
  — disorder format criteria are organized by personality disorder

Source
Psychological Assessment Resource, Inc. (see p. 126)

Schedule of Nonadaptive and Adaptive Personality (SNAP)

Author: Clark LA, 1993

Synopsis
- Consists of 375 true/false items intended to assess trait dimensions in personality disorders
- 34 scales, including
  - 12 trait scales (e.g., mistrust, aggression, dependency)
  - 3 temperament scales (negative temperament, positive temperament, disinhibition)
  - 6 validity scales
  - 13 diagnostic scales: paranoid, schizoid, schizotypal, antisocial, borderline, histrionic, narcissistic, avoidant, dependent, obsessive-compulsive, passive-aggressive, sadistic, self-defeating

Source
University of Minnesota Press, Test Division
Mill Place, Suite 290
111 Third Avenue
Minneapolis, MN   55401-2520

Standardized Assessment of Personality (SAP)

Authors: Mann AH, Jenkins R, Cutting JC & Cowen PJ, 1981

Synopsis
• Different from other Axis II interviews in that it depends solely on interviews with those people closest to the subject (must have known the subject for at least 5 years)
• Based on ICD-9 and ICD-10 criteria
• Assesses 8 diagnoses: anxious, histrionic, dependent, dyssocial, paranoid, anankastic, impulsive, and schizoid disorders
• Studies indicate that the SAP compares well to the International Personality Disorder Examination (IPDE)

Source
Institute of Psychiatry at the Maudsley
King's College London
De Crespigny Park, London
United Kingdom   SE5 8AF
Telephone: 44 0 20 7836 5454
Web Address: http://www.iop.kcl.ac.uk/

Structured Clinical Interview for DSM-IV Axis II Personality Disorders (SCID-II)

Authors: First MB, Gibbon M, Spitzer RL, Williams JB & Benjamin LS, 1996

Synopsis
• A semi-structured diagnostic interview designed to assess the DSM-IV Axis II disorders
• For each of the DSM-IV-TR criteria there are typically one or two standard questions; criteria are grouped by diagnosis
• The simplest Axis II interview to administer and interpret

Source:
American Psychiatric Publishing, Inc. (see p. 121)

Structured Interview for DSM-IV Personality Disorders (SIDP-IV)

Authors: Pfohl B, Blum N & Zimmerman M, 1995

Synopsis
• Consists of 160 questions divided into 10 sections/topics
• Sections include interests and activities, close relationships, emotions, disordered perceptions and thinking
• Designed to resemble a clinical interview
• Those questions addressing specific Axis II criteria are not readily obvious, making it more difficult for the subject to alter responses
• Includes an optional section for an "informant" interview (e.g. family/ friends)

Source
American Psychiatric Publishing, Inc. (see p. 121)

Structured Interview for the Five-Factor Model of Personality (SIFFM)

Authors: Trull TJ & Widiger TA, 1997

Synopsis
- Consists of 120 items
- Focus is on maladaptive components of personality
- Assesses the 5 personality domains of the Five-Factor Model: Neuroticism/Emotional Stability, Extraversion/Introversion, Openness to Experience/Closedness to Experience, Agreeableness/Antagonism, and Conscientiousness/Negligence
- Modeled closely after the NEO PI-R and these assessments may be used together

Source
Psychological Assessment Resources, Inc. (see p. 126)

Wisconsin Personality Disorders Inventory (WISPI)

Authors: Klein MH, Benjamin LS, Rosenfeld RR, Treece C, Husted J & Greist JH, 1993

Synopsis
• Consists of a self-report questionnaire derived from an interpersonal perspective
• Item content is based on the DSM criteria for Axis II disorders
• Items are rated by the subject on a 10 point scale (1= never or not at all true; 10= always or extremely true)
• The WISPI-IV is the most recent version of the original, although most of the items have remained constant over the course of the 3 editions

Source
Dr. Marjorie H. Klein
Department of Psychiatry
Wisconsin Psychiatric Institute and Clinics
6001 Research Park Boulevard
Madison, WI 53719-1179
Telephone: 1-608-263-6066
Fax: 1-608-263-2504
E-mail: mhklein@facstaff.wisc.edu

6.4 Diagnostic Interviews

Psychiatric diagnoses are made with the information that is available clinically. While other branches of medicine have the physical examination and investigations, psychiatry has the interview and mental status examination. This has prompted the use of standardized sets of questions, often called interview schedules, to help assist with the diagnostic assessment. These occur as structured, semi-structured, or checklist schedules. Many of these diagnostic assessments require the interviewer to be trained in administering and scoring the results, and some can involve considerable amounts of time. The instruments listed previously in this chapter generally assess for the full range of personality disorders, there are interviews that evaluate the presence and severity of individual disorders:

- **Dependent Personality Questionnaire** (Tyrer, 2004)
- **Diagnostic Interview for Narcissism** (Gunderson, 1990)
- **Psychopathy Checklist — Revised** (Hare, 1980)
- **Schedule for Schizotypal Personalities** (Baron, 1981)

6.5 References

Gunderson JG, Ronningstam E & Bodkin A
The diagnostic interview for narcissistic patients.
Archives of General Psychiatry 47: p. 676-680, 1990

Hare RD
A research scale for the assessment of psychopathy in criminal populations.
Personality and Individual Differences 1: p. 111-119, 1980

Murphy KR & Davidshofer CO
Psychological Testing: Principles & Applications
Prentice Hall, Englewood Cliffs, NJ, 1988

Rogers R
Handbook of Diagnostic and Structured Interviewing
The Guilford Press, New York, 2001

Tyrer P, Morgan J & Cicchetti D
The dependent personality questionnaire (DPQ): a screening instrument for dependent personality.
International Journal of Social Psychiatry 50(1): p. 10-17, 2004

Baron M, Asnis L & Gruen R
The schedule for schizotypal personalities (SSP): a diagnostic interview for schizotypal features.
Psychiatry Res 4(2): p. 213-28, 1981

Chapter 7

Personality Changes in Later Life

7.1   Introduction

The elderly are becoming North America's fastest growing age group. Estimates for the American population indicate 12.5% were over the age of 65 years in 1990. This group consumes over 30% of health services. While up to 25% of this population suffers from some form of diagnosable mental illness, they receive only about 7% of inpatient psychiatric services and community/private practice services. Goldstein (1991) makes the cogent point that this group is estimated to receive half of the prescriptions written for benzodiazepines and other sedatives, and may have less overall monitoring of their medications that younger groups. The study of how personality disorders change over time is certainly an intriguing one, but an area that has received considerably less attention than other research interests. Some of the reasons for this are thought to be related to:

- Difficulties in sorting out normal reactions to aging from the evolution of a personality disorder.
- The applicability of Axis II diagnostic criteria to this age group
- The continual modification of diagnostic criteria make longitudinal studies difficult; for example, a fifteen-year study initiated in 1979 would have used DSM-II criteria to conduct protocols, which would hardly be applicable to DSM-IV criteria established in 1994
- Other diagnoses (e.g. depression, anxiety disorders) that have a higher morbidity and involve the majority of research efforts
- Difficulties in obtaining accurate epidemiological surveys
- The pessimism in some circles of the efficacy for treating elderly personality disordered patients

7.2   DSM-IV-TR Description of Personality Disorders

The DSM-IV-TR general diagnostic criteria for a personality disorder Criterion D states that "*The pattern is stable and of long duration and its onset can be traced back to at least adolescence or early adulthood.*" (Source: DSM-IV-TR, p. 689)

Personality disorders can be diagnosed in children or adolescents when it appears that maladaptive traits are pervasive, persistent and not related to a major clinical disorder or developmental stage. In order to diagnose a personality disorder in an adolescent, symptoms meeting the diagnostic criteria should be present for at least one year. It is widely recognized that personality disorders are most prevalent in the 25 - 44 year age group. The apparent onset of a personality disorder beyond this age should prompt a thorough investigation for a general medical condition or substance use disorder.

7.3 Difficulties in Using DSM-IV-TR Axis II Criteria

The DSM-IV-TR stipulates that the diagnosis of a personality disorder takes into account an individual's long-term pattern of functioning and that particular personality features must be evident by early adulthood. Unfortunately, there is no time frame given regarding the duration symptoms must be present in order to be considered a diagnosis.

The DSM-IV-TR also does not make a provision for late-onset personality disorders, or the opposite situation involving the attenuation of Axis II symptoms over time (i.e. past personality disorders). Loranger (1987) has suggested that criteria should be met for a five-year time period in order to make the diagnosis of a personality disorder.

It is crucial to assess personality symptoms in a geriatric context. Abrams (1987) found that there were a wide range of Axis II symptoms displayed in elderly populations, though few people met the full criteria for a particular disorder. In particular, the elderly have different social and occupational roles, so it becomes quite difficult to apply these "tests" in deciding if certain behaviors warrant being called disorders.

Abrams (1990) points out the shortcomings of using dimensional (e.g. trait) or categorical (i.e. discrete diagnoses) models in the elderly. Because of the multifactorial changes that occur in aging, current DSM-IV-TR constructs may not be valid descriptions. For example, diagnoses more applicable for the elderly might involve a depressive, euphoric, and a hypochondriacal personality disorder.

Furthermore, the elderly do not have the same energy or opportunities to behave in the ways outlined in the DSM-IV-TR criteria. Promiscuity, shoplifting, binge eating and impulse buying are less likely to be the ways that the geriatric population would demonstrate character pathology.

Similarly, reduced energy, fewer social opportunities, repeated thefts and chronic pain would certainly influence a patient's behavior and could spuriously be mistaken for symptoms of a personality disorder.

McHugh (1983) proposes that a meaningful model be constructed for individual patients involving investigating symptom formation due to situations and vulnerabilities occurring in the second half of life. Research is also being conducted into biological markers (e.g. enzyme levels) which can provide a standardized means of assessment.

7.4   Adult Psychological Development

While physical growth (height anyway) ends with the onset of adulthood, emotional and psychological growth is by no means over. With time and experience, genetic or constitutional factors have a greater time period to be modified by environmental influences. Consequently, personality is not a static entity, but continues to evolve. Erikson outlined the three developmental tasks of adulthood as being:

Intimacy vs. Isolation
The primary task in early adulthood is to establish and maintain an enduring closeness to other adults (outside of the family of origin). Intellectual and emotional maturity continues to develop with the aim of social integration.

Generativity vs. Self-Absorption
Generativity in this stage is usually manifested in guiding and providing for future generations. This is can be directed towards one's children or to society in general through various organizations.

Integrity vs. Despair
Acceptance of one's life path is a key aspect to this stage. Integrity involves a sense of having made a satisfying contribution. However, there are few resources available for developing integrity and, unique to this stage, no clear goal to aspire towards. At this point in time, physical capabilities are declining, illnesses become more severe, and one's peer group diminishes due to relocation, debilitation and death.

Developmental tasks in later life involved disengagement from established social and occupational roles. One measure of psychologically healthy elderly patients has been the acceptance of their inevitable death at earlier ages. Reactions in patients less accepting of this fate involve phobias, paranoia and sleep difficulties

Traits That Become More Pronounced With Time
- Introversion
- Hypochondriasis
- Depression

Traits That Become Less Pronounced With Time
- Impulsivity
- Sociopathy
- Hostility

7.5   Personality Changes in Older Age
Bienenfeld (1990) points out that one of the dominant tasks in later life is to acknowledge one's own mortality. While the elderly do not lose their generosity or caring for others, there is often a notable

degree of self-concern, which can be mistaken for narcissism. At later stages in life, many milestones have been passed and life obligations fulfilled. People no longer have the commitments that took their time and energy earlier in life, so they have the opportunity to focus on themselves. As Richard Gere aptly expressed this in the movie *Primal Fear*, when, regarding people who save for a rainy day, he said *"Well, it's raining."* Often free of social or career restrictions, the elderly are able to invest their money, efforts and concerns in the here and now. Additionally, a sense of entitlement, grandiose sense of self-importance a belief that one's problems are not unique are common enough that these behaviors alone should not constitute narcissistic personality disorder (Abrams, 1990).

Bienenfeld (1990) makes the observation that the above forces of narcissism combined with a growing sense of "finitude" contribute to the almost universal behavior of the elderly in sharing reminiscences. Abrams (1990) notes that emotional exaggeration and an excessively impressionistic style of speaking which lacks detail has been frequently noted among elderly individuals. It is recommended that features other than these be present before considering a diagnosis of HPD.

The high prevalence of mood symptoms in the elderly is an important consideration in the diagnosis of a personality disorder. Differentiating between personality traits and the symptoms of depression is a clinical challenge. For example, dependency, feelings of helplessness, exaggeration of somatic complaints and suicidal ideation are observed in elderly depressed patients and those with personality disorders. Patients who develop depressive episodes later in life have a greater chance of experiencing an incomplete recovery. The persistence of mild to moderate depressive symptoms raises the clinical dilemma about whether a mood disorder with prominent character pathology is present, or a personality disorder was present initially and the patient has gone on to develop secondary mood symptoms.

Abrams (1990) notes that depression in the elderly complicates the assessment of personality by causing cognitive distortions, inaccurate reporting, and modification of character traits. He suggests that in the face of depressive symptoms, personality disorders should be diagnosed sparingly.

7.6   What is the Longitudinal Course of Personality Disorders?

It is important to keep in mind that each person is the product of unique biological, social and psychological circumstances. Two patients with the same personality disorder in the same degree of severity may well have taken very different paths that lead to a common cluster of behaviors. It is therefore very difficult to generalize about whether a particular patient will exhibit the same interpersonal patterns at age twenty, forty and sixty. Life experiences can worsen some symptoms, improve others, or cause the emersion of behaviors later in life that were not seen earlier. In general, traits of personality disordered patients have been found to stable over time. This is supported by psychodynamic/environmental viewpoint in that personality is usually deemed to be formed after a critical period in life. The finding of long-term trait persistence is also supported by the genetic/constitution viewpoint because these are either unchangeable (genetics) or need therapy to modify (e.g. behavior therapy). Cluster B Personality Disorders appear to change most with time because they involve the greatest amount of energy to maintain.

Personality Disorders That Tend to Diminish With Time
- Antisocial
- Borderline
- Histrionic
- Narcissistic
- Passive-Aggressive

Personality Disorders That Tend to Persist With Time
- Avoidant
- Dependent
- Obsessive-Compulsive
- Paranoid
- Schizoid
- Schizotypal

7.7   Treatment Planning for Elderly Patients

Diagnosis

Before a diagnosis can be accurately made, a number of factors need to be considered:

- Concurrent Axis I disorders need to be identified and treated before personality pathology can be ascertained.
- Flexibility will need to be applied to many DSM-IV-TR diagnostic criteria to make them applicable to elderly patients.
- Collateral and longitudinal history is very important to obtain.
- Be particularly wary of late-onset personality disorders, especially if all or many of the symptoms are not typical for the patient

Psychotherapy

Psychotherapy with elderly patients clearly needs to involve less ambitious goals than with younger patients. A lifetime of pathological relationships, disappointments, unstable behavior, etc. often accompanies patients in therapy. With the decline in energy and various physical functions patients do not have the same resources and outlets to with frustration. Somatization becomes more common in the elderly as a means of expression emotional upset. In general, supportive approaches are advocated — the therapist should try to break down barriers and maintain a relationship with the patient.

Pharmacotherapy

Geriatric patients often receive large numbers of prescription medication. This situation is compounded when they see several specialists and/or do not consistently see the same general practitioner. It is not unusual for patients to be taking between twelve and twenty different medications. A rule of thumb is that if someone is on eight or more medications, there is a high likelihood of a drug-drug interaction. Iatrogenic illnesses also become more likely with a higher number of medications.

The four main processes involved in medication distribution are: absorption, distribution, metabolism and elimination. All of these processes are affected by age (e. g. due to reduced blood flow, slowed metabolism, etc.). Psychiatric medications are usually highly lipophilic (become absorbed in fatty tissues). With age, the percentage of body fat increases, so that medications have a greater volume of distribution in the body. In general, dosages for elderly patients are started in the range of one-third to one-half the usual adult amount, with increases being made slowly. Because medication usually is usually has a secondary or adjunctive role in the treatment of personality disorders, particular discretion should be exercised with elderly patients.

7.8   Personality and the Process of Change

The study of personality encompasses a vast area of research and a voluminous body of literature. The issue of which factors influence personality, in which direction, and to what degree, has the subject of intense debate. Methodologically sound research findings report widely disparate result on whether personality changes or remains stable. Evidence abounds to support either finding, depending on what is being measured and what specific definitions are being used.

Weinberger (1994) notes at the end of an entire book on the topic of personality change that there appears to be widespread agreement that personality remains flexible and can change until about the age of thirty. Beyond this age, there is less of a consensus, though some studies report that considerable change occurs throughout adulthood.

Examining this issue further, Weinberger (1994) delineates which factors are likely to change and which are likely to remain stable. Returning to the issue of temperament, Costa & McCrea (1990) factor analyzed five key qualities or basic tendencies (often referred to as **the big five**) that remain stable after the age of thirty.

"CANOE"

- Conscientiousness
- Agreeableness
- Neuroticism
- Openness to experience
- Extroversion

Costa & McCrea (1990) indicate that despite the relative stability of these basic tendencies, their expression, called **characteristic adaptations**, can and will change throughout adulthood. McAdams (1994) developed the following model of personality structure:

Level 1 Basic tendencies	Largely independent of environmental influence; remains stable over time
Level 2 Characteristic adaptations	Habits, attitudes, relationships, interests, etc.; these change with time
Level 3 Existential personality	This is how the person defines him or herself; this constantly evolves as the person seeks change from within

7.9 Personality and the Process of Psychotherapy

The preceding section focused on the stability in personality with life events and the passage of time. This is a different set of observations than for people who engage in psychotherapy to seek change. Eysenk (1952) challenged the efficacy of psychotherapy, resulting in a huge volume of work being done not only on outcome studies, but the process of how change is effected. Starting with the work of Smith (1980), it has generally been accepted that psychotherapy is effective and that patients are better off receiving treatment than not. Weinberger (1994) also sums up a considerable literature by saying that there is no form of therapy which is clearly superior to others. Weinberger (1994) and Bandura (1961) then attempt to delineate the factors involved in therapeutic change:

Bandura
- Counter-conditioning
- Extinction
- Discrimination learning
- Reinforcement of desired behaviors
- Punishment of undesirable behaviors
- Imitation of role model

Weinberger
- Working through the transference
- Developing a working alliance
- Exposure to the source of interpersonal difficulty and mastery of these situations
- Attribution of improvement to to the self rather than therapist

It is still a matter of debate as to whether personality itself changes or the person learns to function more adaptively. Either way, evidence from the literature, anecdotal reports and clinical lore report the therapy is effective, and in many cases depends most strongly on the skills possessed, and interest shown by, the therapist.

7.10   References

Abrams RC, Alexopoulos GS & Young RC
Geriatric depression and DSM-III-R personality disorder criteria.
Journal of the American Geriatric Society 35: p. 383-386, 1987

Abrams RC
Personality Disorders in the Elderly in Verwoerdt's Clinical Geropsychiatry,
3ʳᵈ Edition
Williams & Wilkins, Baltimore, 1990

American Psychiatric Association
**Diagnostic & Statistical Manual of Mental Disorders, Fourth Edition, Text
Revision**
American Psychiatric Association, Arlington, VA, 2000

Bandura A
Psychotherapy as a learning process.
Psychological Bulletin 58: 143-159, 1961

Bienenfeld D
Psychology of Aging in Verwoerdt's Clinical Geropsychiatry, 3ʳᵈ Edition
Williams & Wilkins, Baltimore, 1990

Costa, PT & McCrea RR
Personality in Adulthood
The Guilford Press, New York, 1990

Davidson J
Pharmacological Treatment, in
Textbook of Geriatric Psychiatry, 2ⁿᵈ Edition
Busse EW & Blazer DG, Editors
American Psychiatric Press, Inc., Washington DC, 1996

Erik H. Erikson EH
Identity and the Life Cycle
W.W. Norton, New York, 1994

Eysenk HJ
The effect of psychotherapy: an evaluation
Journal of Consulting Psychology 16: p. 319-324, 1952

Goldstein MZ
Evaluation of the Elderly Patient in Verwoerdt's Clinical Geropsychiatry, 3ʳᵈ
Edition
Williams & Wilkins, Baltimore, 1990

Loranger AW, Susman VL, Oldham, JM & Russakoff LM
The personality disorder examination: a preliminary report.
J Pers 1: p. 1-13, 1987

McAdams DP
Can Personality Change? Levels of Stability and Growth in Personality Across the Lifespan, in
Can Personality Change?
Heatherton TF & Weinberger JL, Editors
American Psychological Association, Washington, DC, 1994

McHugh PR & Slavney PR
The Perspectives of Psychiatry
The Johns Hopkins University Press, Baltimore, 1983

Smith ML, Glass GV & Miller FI
The Benefits of Psychotherapy
Johns Hopkins University Press, Baltimore, 1980

Weinberger JL
Can Personality Change? in
Can Personality Change?
Heatherton TF & Weinberger JL, Editors
American Psychological Association, Washington, DC, 1994

Chapter 8

Other Personality Topics

8.1 Multiple Personality Disorder/ Dissociative Identity Disorder

Introduction

Multiple personality disorder (MPD) was renamed the **dissociative identity disorder (DID)** starting with the DSM-IV. The essential feature is the co-existence of two or more distinct identities, or personalities that take control of an individual and cause deficits in the recall of information.

Some key names associated with development of this disorder are:
- Eugène Azam (France, 1850's) — described the symptoms of multiple personality disorder in a patient named Félida X
- Pierre Janet (France, 1880's) — conceptualized and investigated the process of dissociation.

- Freud and Breuer (1883-85) — proposed a model of mental functioning where traumatic memories were kept out of conscious awareness by repression, as seen in their famous case, Anna O.
- Morton Prince (1906) — wrote an account of a patient with several personalities called *"The Dissociation of a Personality."*

MPD is not considered a disorder of personality, but is included for its heuristic value. It is categorized as a **dissociative disorder** and has historically been classified under **hysterical neuroses, dissociative type.** Renaming this condition re-emphasizes the psychological process producing the different identities (dissociation), rather than the observable manifestations (multiple personalities). The term implies that a single person manifests different internal and external experiences of the self.

DID is a fascinating condition, in which the varying identities or "alters" can be sufficiently well-defined to be considered separate "personalities." The alters can have distinct: names, sexual identities, sexual orientation, voices, facility with foreign languages, handedness and handwriting. Amazingly, each can have distinct illnesses, EEGs, eyeglass prescriptions and even allergies! The usual arrangement involves a dominant personality that is aware of all of the fragments, though this is not always the personality that seeks treatment. Alters appear to be variably aware of one another. The total number of personalities has been reported to exceed fifty, with the average being in the range of ten to twelve. Frequently, the personalities have some connection with one another. For example, all of the persons involved in a traumatic episode (victim, perpetrator, witness, etc.) can be embodied by different personalities. Also, dichotomous personalities (e.g. a good/evil pairing) are often present.

Media Examples

Multiple personality themes have often involved the duality of human nature. A classic example is Robert Louis Stevenson's *Dr. Jekyll and Mr. Hyde*, which has been made into several movie versions. Many other movies and books have been constructed around this theme. Movie versions have been made from real cases, in particular:

The Three Faces of Eve

This is book by Drs. Thigpen and Cleckley (the same Cleckley who wrote *The Mask of Sanity*). Interestingly, Morton Prince's book recorded the case of a Miss Beauchamp, whose three personalities were referred to as "the Saint, the Devil, and the Woman." These are the same three manifestations of the character played by Joanne Woodward, who won an Academy Award for her performance.

Etiology/Presumed Etiology

Biological

- Epilepsy or head injuries are present in up to a quarter of patients
- Evoked potentials show clear characteristics for each personality
- Non-dominant temporal lobe dysfunction may be present
- Mood symptoms are often present in the host personality
- A genetic component may contribute to higher familial incidence

Psychosocial

- Frequent history of **imaginary companions** as children
- In almost all cases, severe psychological, physical, or sexual abuse, or some other traumatic event occurred
- Absence of support from significant others is thought to contribute to the extensive use of dissociation to cope with trauma

Differential Diagnosis

Axis I

- Schizophrenia
- Other dissociative disorders
- Posttraumatic stress disorder (PTSD)
- Mood disorder (e.g. bipolar — rapid cycling or psychotic features)
- Substance use disorders (especially involving hallucinogens)

Axis II

- Borderline personality disorder

Axis III/Other

- Brain tumors
- Malingering/factitious disorder
- Epilepsy, especially temporal lobe/partial complex seizures

The Dissociative Self

Childhood sexual abuse, and in particular ritual or cult abuse is the most common etiologic factor in DID. The child however, has a constitutional predisposition to use dissociation as a defense, as several other reactions are seen (repression, denial, acting out, identification with the aggressor, substance abuse, etc.). McWilliams (1994) notes that individuals who have a rich fantasy life, a penchant for imaginative play, and a talent for creativity are more likely to dissociate under the overwhelming stress of trauma or abuse. Ross (1989) hypothesizes a cognitive map as follows:

The primary personality cannot handle the memories
↓
The primary personality is responsible for the abuse
↓
It is wrong to be angry about the abuse
↓
Different parts of the self become separate selves
↙ ↘

- I never feel angry; she is the bad one
- She deserves to be punished for being angry
- I love my parents; she hates them

- I must be bad; this wouldn't have happened otherwise
- I deserve to be punished for being angry
- I can't trust myself or anyone else

Comment on MPD/DID

The apparent prevalence of this disorder has increased dramatically in recent years. This may well be due to an increased awareness and sensitivity to dissociative states on the part of therapists. It is at time very difficult to distinguish between the defenses of splitting and dissociation, which lead to different diagnostic impressions.

On the other hand, this epidemic has sparked considerable controversy, as well as evidence of improperly made diagnoses (Merskey, 1992). The diagnosis of MPD may well carry a reduced expectation for taking responsibility for one's actions, making this condition attractive to impulsive characters and malingerers.

8.2 Masochistic (Self-Defeating) & Sadistic Personalities

The Masochistic (Self-Defeating) Personality

The term **masochism** derives from the writings of Leopold von Sacher Masoch (1836-1895). He was an Austrian novelist whose works contained characters who derived sexual pleasure from being hurt, abused, or humiliated. When the term is used in a sexual context, it is called **erotogenic** or **primary masochism**. Freud used the term **moral masochism** to refer to behavior that was self-damaging, which is the focus of most psychiatric literature. Masochistic patients are notable for repeating self-damaging relationships (**repetition-compulsion**). Many other writers have described this type of personality, including Krafft-Ebing (1882/1937), Reich (1933), and Kernberg (1988). DSM-III-R included **self-defeating personality**

disorder in the appendix as a disorder requiring further study. It was not validated as a discrete personality disorder and was dropped from the DSM-IV-TR. Masochistic behavior itself is common and not necessarily pathological. Suffering for some greater gain, or for the benefit of others, has a good in common with the ego defense of **altruism**, or more specifically, **altruistic surrender.** Self-defeating behavior is manifested as being: accident-prone, self-injurious, martyr-like and self-righteous. Masochism may develop as a strategy to secure or perpetuate attachment. Being punished or teased may have been the only emotional connection a child had with caregivers. A common cognition in this disorder is that "an abusive relationship is better than no relationship at all." Masochistic behavior can be conceived as a blend of **depressive** and **paranoid** behavior. While patients may feel worthless, they retain the hope that this quality will bring sympathy and care from others. They share the same perception of threat as paranoid patients, but instead, attack themselves to ward off an attempt by others to do so.

The Sadistic Personality

The term **sadism** is named after the French writer Marquis de Sade (1740-1814). It was initially used to refer to people who derived erotic pleasure from inflicting cruelty on others. In a more generalized sense, sadistic behavior involves the enjoyment of inflicting physical violence, pain, humiliation and harsh discipline onto others. Frequently, sadistic patients were brutalized as children. This disorder is thought to result from an amalgamation of sexual and aggressive drives.

The **sadistic personality disorder** also appeared in the appendix of DSM-III-R, but was similarly not included in DSM-IV-TR. Sadistic behavior is a large component of the observed behavior in **antisocial personalities**, and to a lesser extent, **passive-aggressive** personalities. Sexual sadism is diagnosed as a **paraphilia**, a type of sexual disorder. Descriptions of a **sadomasochistic personality disorder** exist, reflecting the coexistence of both elements in patients. This is in keeping with the observation that most intrapsychic states exist with their opposite. Many examples of sadomasochism can be seen in the performing arts. Treatment involves psychotherapy, where patients can become aware of their aggressive impulses and fear of/need for punishment.

8.3 The Organic Personality/Personality Change Due to a General Medical Condition

Organic personality disorder is an antiquated but still common term used to denote a character change due to an identifiable illness or incident. In a neurological sense, the brain is a passive victim of the disease processes in other organs. Adding to this sympathetic view is the sad reality that neurons in the central nervous system (brain and spinal cord) do not regenerate themselves after an insult. The most common conditions causing personality changes are:

Mnemonic — "PAST THEME"

Poisoning (especially heavy metals)	Trauma
AIDS/Neurosyphilis	Huntington's disease
Stroke (Cerebrovascular disorders)	Epilepsy
Tumors	Multiple Sclerosis
	Endocrine disorders

Some cerebral insults affect many cognitive processes (intelligence, memory, coordination, etc.). Other lesions affect personality almost exclusively, with preservation of most other cerebral functions. Most examples of this phenomenon involve the frontal lobes of the brain. Known as the **frontal lobe syndrome**, Lishman (1998) lists the most common characterologic changes as: reduced volition and social awareness, reduced tact and restraint, mildly euphoric mood, irritable outbursts and impaired judgment. In general, there is a coarsening of personality features and an accentuation of pre-existing traits.

Changes range from subtle to marked. In the majority of cases, patients are unaware of their alteration in personality. While damage to specific parts of the frontal lobes appear to cause particular findings, injury to both frontal lobes (usually due to trauma) is particularly worrisome.

Parker (1996) identifies a condition known as the **cerebral personality disorder** involving changes in mood, motivation and affective expression following brain trauma. This term indicates that certain brain centers (e.g. limbic system, prefrontal cortex) may be even more responsible for personality changes than the frontal lobes. A fuller description of personality changes due to brain insults is as follows:

- Disturbance in emotional control
- Impulsivity
- Uncertain identity
- Reduced confidence/self-esteem
- Substance abuse
- Inability to learn from experience
- Reduced motivation
- Social withdrawal
- Angry outbursts
- Diminished insight
- Somatization
- Insecurity/paranoia

Personality changes due to frontal lobe injury can be difficult to diagnose because damage is usually diffuse and will not be visualized on neuroimaging. Also, there are no incontrovertible neuropsychological measurements of frontal lobe dysfunction. Lastly, other formal tests of cognitive abilities can remain unaffected by insults which affect personality. Lishman (1998) notes than on occasion, there have been improvements in personality function following mild to moderate head injury, namely reduced anxiety and increased sociability.

A number of Axis I disorders can arise due to head injuries: PTSD, OCD, phobic disorders, mood disorders, psychotic disorders, somatoform disorders and dissociative disorders. There is also an appreciable risk of suicide.

8.4   The Inadequate Personality

The inadequate personality disorder was included in DSM-I and DSM-II. The hallmark of this disorder is an ineffectual response to day-to-day demands and the expectations of others. While patients are aware of their shortcomings, they have neither the desire nor the resources to change. They see their low level of achievement as part of their nature, and in this sense, it is egosyntonic.

Other characteristics include:
• Poor social judgment and adjustment
• Low level of occupational performance and frequent job changes
• Lack of stamina (physical, mental and emotional)
• Low level of adaptation to societal demands
• Poor ability to plan for the future

This description of this personality has an overlap with the criteria for **dependent, avoidant** and **schizoid** personalities.

8.5 The Asthenic Personality

The asthenic personality disorder appeared only in DSM-II. The word asthenia derives from the Greek word for *weakness*. The term is still used to describe someone of slight build or body structure.

The main features of this personality are:
- Lassitude, lethargy, lack of will (abulia)
- Lack of enthusiasm and the capacity for enjoyment (anhedonia)
- Inability to withstand average/expectable stresses

This description shares considerable overlap with the features of **depression** and the **negative symptoms of schizophrenia**. This disorder was thought to have a constitutional origin. A more acute "neurasthenic neurosis" has been described, which may now be considered an **adjustment disorder**. An of this personality type can be seen in the H.T. Webster character called Caspar Milquetoast, from the comic strip called *The Timid Soul*. The word "milquetoast" refers to one who is easily dominated or intimidated.

8.6 The Cyclothymic Personality

The **cyclothymic personality disorder** was included in the DSM-I and DSM-II. The hallmark of this disorder was a fluctuation in mood that occurred on a regular basis and was serious enough to affect functioning. In the DSM-III, this condition became the cyclothymic disorder, a type of affective disorder. In the DSM-IV-TR, it is still listed under this name; however, the category is now called **mood disorders**.

The disorder resembles **bipolar mood disorder** except the mood symptoms occur with smaller amplitude. The "highs" are hypomanic (not manic), and the "lows" do not meet the criteria for a **major depressive episode**.

8.7 The Explosive Personality

The **explosive personality disorder** burst onto the scene only in the DSM-II, though the DSM-I had a category called the emotionally unstable personality. This has also been referred to as the **epileptoid personality disorder**. This diagnosis was given to patients who had volatile emotional responses to minor upsets. When incited, patients raged with verbal barrages and physical destructiveness.

This disorder was reclassified in the DSM-III as the **intermittent explosive disorder**. In appears in the DSM-IV-TR as an impulse-control disorder. The DSM-IV-TR criteria emphasize occurrence of physical assault or destruction of property.

This disorder was changed to an Axis I condition because the loss of control was not typical behavior for patients. Additionally, it was egodystonic. However, the inter-episode personality characteristics have been variably described. Some patients were described as well-adjusted, pleasant and calm. Aberrations were only seen upon provocation with seemingly minor events. Other patients appeared to have aggressive, defiant, caustic and provocative features that were consistently seen between explosive episodes. These patients may be better accounted for by the diagnoses of **antisocial personality disorder** or **narcissistic personality disorder** (when experiencing a narcissistic rage), in addition to the intermittent explosive disorder.

Movie Example

Barry Egan (Adam Sandler) is the owner of a business that sells novelty toilet plungers, called fungers. Barry is a lonely man who seems to be immersed in self-loathing. He has seven sisters who make him the constant focus of their attention, particularly with phone calls. Barry comes across as a likeable and decent guy who in many instances seems patient and composed.

However, at certain times in the film he engages in fits of violence. Ironically, it is being teased about previous episodes of losing control that seem to set him off again. When Barry is on a date with Lena (Emily Watson), she casually brings up something that one of his sisters said. He calmly excuses himself and then wildly trashes the restaurant bathroom, leading to a large repair bill. In another scene, Barry kicks in a sliding glass door after receiving very little provocation to do so.

8.8 References

American Psychiatric Association
Diagnostic and Statistical Manual of Mental Disorders, 4th Edition, Text Revision
American Psychiatric Association, Arlington, VA, 2000

American Psychiatric Association
Diagnostic and Statistical Manual of Mental Disorders, 4th Edition
American Psychiatric Association, Washington, DC, 1994

American Psychiatric Association
Diagnostic and Statistical Manual of Mental Disorders, 3rd Edition, Revised
American Psychiatric Association, Washington, DC, 1987

American Psychiatric Association
Diagnostic and Statistical Manual of Mental Disorders, 3rd Edition
American Psychiatric Association, Washington, DC, 1980

American Psychiatric Association
Diagnostic and Statistical Manual of Mental Disorders, 2nd Edition
American Psychiatric Association, Washington, DC, 1968

American Psychiatric Association
Diagnostic and Statistical Manual of Mental Disorders
American Psychiatric Association, Washington, DC, 1952

Beck AT, Freeman A, Davis DD & Associates
Cognitive Therapy of Personality Disorders, 2nd Edition
The Guilford Press, New York, 2003

Freedman A, Kaplan H & Sadock B, Editors
Comprehensive Textbook of Psychiatry, 2nd Edition
Williams & Wilkins, Baltimore, 1975

Kaplan H & Sadock B, Editors
Comprehensive Textbook of Psychiatry, 5th Edition
Williams & Wilkins, Baltimore, 1989

Kaplan H & Sadock B, Editors
Synopsis of Psychotherapy, 8th Edition
Williams & Wilkins, Baltimore, 1998

Kernberg O
Clinical dimensions of mashochism.
Journal of the American Psychoanalytic Association 36: p. 1005-1029, 1988

Krafft-Ebing R
Psychopathia Sexualis
Physicians & Surgeons Books, New York, 1882/1937

Lishman WA
Organic Psychiatry: The Psychological Consequences of Cerebral Disorder, 3rd Edition
Blackwell Science, London, England, 1998

McWilliams N
Psychoanalytic Diagnosis
The Guilford Press; New York, 1994

Merskey H
The manufacture of personalities: the production of mpd.
British Journal of Psychiatry 160: p. 327, 1992

Parker RS
The spectrum of emotional distress and personality changes after minor head injury incurred in a motor vehicle accident.
Brain Injury 10(4): p. 287-302, 1996

Pies R
Clinical Manual of Psychiatric Diagnosis and Treatment
American Psychiatric Press; Washington, DC, 1994

Reich W
Character Analysis
Farrar, Strauss & Giroux, New York, 1933

Ross CA
Multiple Personality Disorder: Diagnosis, Clinical Features & Treatment
Wiley & Sons, New York, 1989

Chapter 9

Personality Disorder Humor

The Schizoid Personality

Biographical Information

Name: G.O. Solo
Occupation: Toll booth collector between 1 and 7 a.m.
Appearance: Stove-pipe pants, and a circa 1970's ultra-wide tie
Relationship with animals: Brings "best friend" to session
Favorite Songs: *Alone Again, Naturally; Solitaire*
Motto: Through email I will prevail

At the Therapist's Office

Before Session: Gets first appointment to avoid seeing others in the waiting room
Waiting Room Reading: Reads *Statistics Quarterly* in the hallway
During Session: Plays *Hide & Seek*; only won't seek
Fantasies Involve: Liaison with philosophy course instructor

Relationship with Therapist: Asks to play *Dungeons & Dragons*
Behavior During Session: Teeters on the edge. . . of the chair
Brings to Session: Collection of mail-order catalogs

The Paranoid Personality

Biographical Information

Name: Perry Noyd
Occupation: Full-time movie projectionist
Appearance: Wears glasses with rear-view mirrors
Relationship with animals: Doubts even his dog's fidelity
Favorite Song: *I Spy* theme song
Motto: In vigilance I trust

At the Therapist's Office

Before Session: Checks to see if he was followed
Waiting Room Reading: Authenticates therapist's diploma
During Session: Questions partner's fidelity
Fantasies Involve: Demanding a full explanation of therapist's jokes
Relationship with Therapist: Questions therapist's fidelity
Behavior During Session: Complains about the lack of warmth in office
Brings to Session: Scrapbook of injustice collection

The Schizotypal Personality

Biographical Information

Name: Aldrina Q. Cosmos

Occupation: Developer for a UFO landing pad

Appearance: Tin foil hat, unpaired socks, mood ring, dress hemmed with staples

Relationship with animals: Laments the fact that pet budgie remains dead, despite séances

Favorite Song: *Dark Side of the Moon*

Motto: There are no strangers, just friends from past lives

At the Therapist's Office

Before Session: Reads palms, tea leaves and tarot cards of others in the waiting room

Waiting Room Reading: *Astrology Weekly*

During Session: Initiates session by talking to herself

Fantasies Involve: A management position with the *Thought Broadcasting Corporation*

Relationship with Therapist: Casts a spell on therapist

Behavior During Session: Plays with Voodoo Barbie doll

Brings to Session: An autographed copy of her new book on neologisms, *"How to Call 'Em as I see 'Em"*

The Histrionic Personality

Biographical Information

Name: Cindi L. Valentine
Occupation: Cosmetician & Aesthetician
Appearance: Coordinated shoes, earrings, purse, nails and accessories
Relationship with animals: Has cats named Puffy, Buffy & Muffy
Favorite Song: *Love Me Tender*
Motto: It's not how you feel, it's how you look!

At the Therapist's Office

Before Session: Flirts with others in the waiting room
Waiting Room Reading: Does quiz from fashion magazine
During Session: Gives quiz results to therapist
Fantasies Involve: Becoming a radio sex therapist
Relationship with Therapist: Writes best-selling novel based on sexual fantasies with therapist
Behavior During Session: Faints when quiz results are interpreted
Brings to Session: Hides a perfumed business card in the seat cushion

173

The Antisocial Personality

Biographical Information

Name: Antonio Alto
Occupation: Arsonist-at-large for local Fire Deptartment
Appearance: Sibeburns, muscle shirt, tattoos
Relationship with animals: Trained dog to snatch purses
Favorite Song: *Criminal Mind*
Motto: I don't mind and you don't matter

At the Therapist's Office

Before Session: Robs pharmacy in the lobby
Waiting Room Reading: Steals magazines; leaves copies of *Playboy*, sans centerfold
During Session: Starts sentences with "!@#$%&*"
Fantasies Involve: Seducing probation officer
Relationship with Therapist: Picks therapist's pocket, takes long-distance phone card
Behavior During Session: Carves up armrest, finds *Histrionic*'s phone number in the seat cushion
Brings to Session: Brochure for a car alarm (that he knows how to dismantle)

The Borderline Personality

Biographical Information

Name: Tara Bull

Occupation: Emotional hotline counselor

Appearance: Dresses entirely in either black or white; today it's black

Relationship with animals: Sleeps with teddy bear and an assortment of stuffed animals

Favorite Song: *Love Rollercoaster*

Motto: Come here! Go away! Come here!

At the Therapist's Office

Before Session: Fights with ex-lover outside office

Waiting Room Reading: Castrates all pictures of men in magazines

During Session: Smells *Histrionic's* perfume and goes into a rage

Fantasies Involve: Ménage with therapist and partner

Relationship with Therapist: Threatens blackmail over above fantasy

Behavior During Session: Widens hole made by *Antisocial*

Brings to Session: Suicide note, with weekly changes

The Narcissistic Personality

Biographical Information

Name: James Pond
Occupation: Window dresser for a fashion store
Appearance: Silk suit, cubic zirconium cufflinks & tie pin, alligator shoes
Relationship with animals: Walks friend's Afghan in order to impress others
Favorite Song: *King of the Road*
Motto: After me, you come first

At the Therapist's Office

Before Session: Preens with a portable mirror
Waiting Room Reading: GQ; tells others he will be featured in the the next issue
During Session: Starts each sentence with, "I . . . "
Fantasies Involve: Wonders what he's like in bed
Relationship with Therapist: Self-appointed fashion consultant
Behavior During Session: Acts as if the session is being filmed
Brings to Session: A discount coupon for his store

The Avoidant Personality

Biographical Information

Name: Mike McMeek
Occupation: Model for "before" pictures in weightlifting ads
Appearance: Matches clothes to office wallpaper
Relationship with animals: Has dog introduces him to others
Favorite Songs: *Born to be Mild; If You Asked Me To*
Motto: I gotta be. . . anyone but me

At the Therapist's Office

Before Session: Followed *Schizoid's* path; hoped they might meet
Waiting Room Reading: Reads nothing so as not to deprive others
During Session: Discusses detours, off-ramps & exits
Fantasies Involve: Reincarnating Dale Carnegie as his uncle
Relationship with Therapist: Protects car from *Antisocial*
Behavior During Session: Spends time with head in lampshade
Brings to Session: *Invisible Man* comic books

The Dependent Personality

Biographical Information

Name: Anita Lott
Occupation: Food Banker & Pet Hotelier
Appearance: *Just Take Me* t-shirt under a big fuzzy sweater
Relationship with animals: Confines dog to prevent elopement
Favorite Song: *Stand By Me*
Motto: Don't leave home without me

At the Therapist's Office

Before Session: Sees another therapist
Waiting Room Reading: Autographed self-help book from yet
another therapist
During Session: Describes nightmares after seeing *Home Alone*
Fantasies Involve: Confining therapist to her home
Relationship with Therapist: Sits in car when **Avoidant** not
there
Behavior During Session: Sits next to therapist; records session
with a portable tape recorder
Brings to Session: Nightly dinner invitation

The Obsessive-Compulsive Personality

Biographical Information

Name: R. Lloyd Micron
Occupation: Molecule counter for a chemical company
Appearance: Starched underwear and socks
Relationship with animals: Has sent dog to obedience school every year for 8 years
Favorite Song: *You'll Do It My Way*
Motto: There are rules about making rules

At the Therapist's Office

Before Session: Washes hands before and after using restroom
Waiting Room Reading: Arranges magazines alphabetically
During Session: Quotes from an etiquette book
Fantasies Involve: Not flushing the toilet
Relationship with Therapist: Repairs hole in chair with pocket sewing kit
Behavior During Session: Demands watches be synchronized
Brings to Session: A bottle of the cologne, *Obsession*

179

Parking Lot of the Personality Disordered

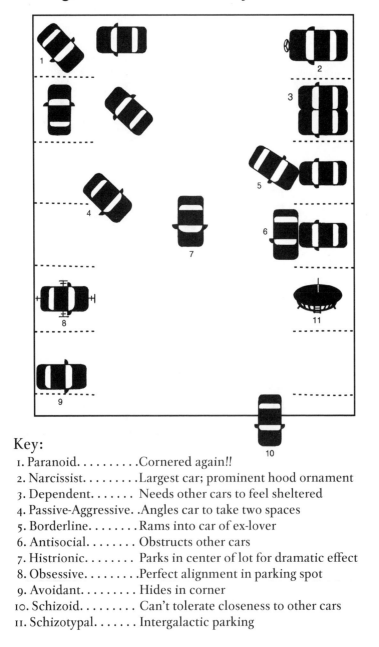

Key:

1. Paranoid. . . . . .Cornered again!!
2. Narcissist. . . . . . . .Largest car; prominent hood ornament
3. Dependent. . . . . . . Needs other cars to feel sheltered
4. Passive-Aggressive. .Angles car to take two spaces
5. Borderline. . . . . . . .Rams into car of ex-lover
6. Antisocial. . . . . Obstructs other cars
7. Histrionic. . . . . Parks in center of lot for dramatic effect
8. Obsessive. . . . . .Perfect alignment in parking spot
9. Avoidant. . . . . Hides in corner
10. Schizoid. . . . . Can't tolerate closeness to other cars
11. Schizotypal. . . . . . . Intergalactic parking

Bistro of the Personality Disordered

1. Paranoid.........Sits with back to the wall; spies on food preparation area when doors swing open
2. Narcissist.........Expects most exclusive table without a reservation; sends entrée back to chef
3. Dependent.......While a vegetarian non-smoker, eats veal and sits in smoking section to please date
4. Passive-Aggressive..Blows smoke into the non-smoking section
5. Borderline.........When informed he won't leave his wife, she throws a drink on her date then stuffs a a cornish hen on his head
6. Antisocial.........Sucker punches waiter and in the resulting confusion steals the tip left by the Narcissist
7. Histrionic.........Does an interpretive belly dance near the jukebox in the center of the restaurant
8. Obsessive.........Visits other tables polishing the crystal, aligning cutlery and giving etiquette tips
9. Avoidant.........Gives tips for service from take-out counter
10. Schizoid.........Orders home delivery; ingests food through a straw sticking out of mail slot
11. Schizotypal.......Eats gardening equipment and a ginsu knife

Why Did the Chicken Really Cross the Road?

Paranoid.	To commit an act of unprovoked aggression.
Schizotypal. . . .	To embark on a new astral plane.
Schizoid.	This was the only kind trip society would let it take on its own.
Antisocial.	If you saw me coming, you'd cross the road too!
Borderline.	It wanted to take out its revenge on Colonel Sanders.
Histrionic.	No one would notice if it just stood there.
Narcissistic. . . .	I know that chicken, I helped her achieve stardom.
Obsessive.	It was the logical next step in avian evolution.
Avoidant.	The chicken crossed the road and that's good enough for me.
Dependent. . . .	It was facing the road less traveled, and that was too much for this chicken.

Personalities 'R Us Corporate Structure

Senior Management

President
Narcissist

Vice-President
Paranoid

Personnel
Borderline

Middle Management

Advertising Histrionic	**Legal Department** Antisocial
Research Schizotypal	**Customer Service** Passive-Aggressive

Workforce (with preferred hours)

Dependent Whenever Told	**Obsessive** Day & Night
Schizoid Nights Only	**Avoidant** Undesirable Shifts

The Mutation of Ego Defenses

In his structural theory of the mind, Freud divided the psychic apparatus into the id, ego and superego. The ego, being the "middle child" in this arrangement, was set up to get nailed from both sides. Strategy dictates that a strong offense starts with a strong defense. Freud appreciated the need for defense mechanisms for the ego, and duly noted repression to be the mother of all defenses. A further cataloging of ego defenses was provided by his daughter Anna, and Valiant[1] efforts have enumerated still more. Just as Freud's Drive Theory was overrun by *Objectionable Relations Theory*[2] and *Selfish Psychology*[3], ego defenses have had to mutate to adjust to contemporary demands.

Narcissisy Defenses

Old: Primitive Idealization   **New:** American Expressization

Explanation: The ultimate expression of "plasticity," allows the ego to function autonomously, at least until the end of the month.

Old: Projective Identification   **New:** Primate Identification
Explanation: Used by over-socialized egos (primarily male) to seek psychic equilibrium through the imitation of primate behavior.

Old: Denial   **New:** Alibido
Explanation: An amalgamation of two other defenses, alibi and libido, with the first is usually covering up the actions of the second.

Post-Premature Defenses

Old: Acting Out   **New:** Acting
Explanation: This allows the ego to make the most of the "as if" personality by assuming identities of fictitious characters. Combined with relocation, this can be a lucrative defense.

Old: Regression   **New:** Digression
Explanation: The spontaneous use of irrelevant and dated material in a rambling and verbose style assures complacency in others.

Old: Passive Aggression   **New:** Passé Aggression
Explanation: Here, the ego becomes embroiled in the social milieu and struggles of a prior decade in order to avoid facing the demands

of the current one. Some decades (particularly the 1960's) seem heavily favored for use with this defense.

Post-Post-Mature Defenses

Old: Controlling   **New:** Remote Controlling
Explanation: The ego is now able to achieve remarkable control over the external environment with this new defense. Not only is it effective with electrical devices, it can cause marked changes in humans as well.

Old: Displacement   **New:** Relocation
Explanation: This defense allows the ego to displace itself across municipal, county and federal lines as a way of avoiding confrontation. It may be that egos using this defense cluster geographically (e.g. Hollywood).

Old: Isolation   **New:** Insulation
Explanation: An evolved defense that now gives the ego materials with which to perform the isolating. The use of urea-formaldehyde insulation was one of the early misapplications of this defense.

Victor Mature Defenses

Old: Humor   **New:** Humor
Explanation: No comment.

Old: Altruism   **New:** Trumanism
Explanation: Plainly stated, this enables the ego to have hard cash, as well as responsibility, seek a final resting place on a desk.

References

[1] Valiant, Prince George: **The Hierarchy of Ego Defenses**
Journal of Medieval Psychology: Round Table Press, New England

[2] Maggie, Melanie and Bill
Driven to Detraction: Objectionable Relations Theory
British School Publishers: United Queendom

[3] Kohutek, Heinz
From Lilliputian to Kohutian: The Advancement of Self Through Selfish Psychology
Chapter 1: *Heinz 57 Manual of Therapeutic Interventions*
Mirror on the Wall Press: New York

Nag-B-Gone®

NAG-B-GONE: *tri-caffeinated-primadonna-adnauseate-turbonagging-hydrazine* — a proprietary brand attitude suppressant

Supplied As:

- Nag-B-Gone™ Regular Strength — 250mg tablets
- Nag-B-Gone™ Extra Strength — 500mg tablets
- Nag-B-Gone™ STAT — 750mg IM blow dart form
- Nag-B-Gone™ PMS — 5g long-acting IM form — monthly injection
- Nag-B-Gone™ EverFlow — 50 g/L intravenous formulation

Indications:
For the reduction of attitude, grandiosity and pomposity in all settings; alleviates demonstrations of superiority and rampant indignation.

Action:
Temporarily deadens attitudinal receptors in the superior portion of the locus narcissisticus in the dominant frontal lobe.

Alternate Forms:

WhineAway®
A mild attitude suppressant in a pleasant-tasting cappuccino-flavored liquid form for those who can't stop talking long enough to take the tablets. Also practical for surreptitious introduction into colleagues' coffee mugs.

DeFlato®
An attitude suppressant in an aerosol form with two delivery modes:
- wide setting works as an antiperspirant
- narrow setting delivers an effective dose across conference rooms

Flock-Off®
A triple-strength formulation available in suppository form. For use in extreme cases, such as meetings composed of multitudes of the individuals listed above (e.g. Narcissists Anonymous).

Narciss-Fix-All®
An experimental community-based formulation suitable for inclusion in water supply; government approval is pending for endemic areas.

If You Love Something, Set It Free . . .

Antisocial.	If it doesn't come back to you, hunt it down and do something undignified.
Schizoid.	So, what's the problem?
Dependent.	And walk right back in the front door.
Obsessive.	By spending a requisite amount of time apart, an emotion may occur.
Narcissistic.	Take this opportunity . . . please!
Histrionic.	A complete make-over is clearly required to rekindle this romance.
Paranoid.	While this person is gone, place bugs in the phones, a hidden camera on all floors, and hire a private investigator.
Schizotypal.	Get your fortune read before returning.

Shopping by Diagnosis

Area/Activity in Store   Diagnosis

Check Out

• Exact-change cashier	Obsessive-Compulsive
• Uses cash register nearest the exit (for a faster getaway)	Antisocial
• Enters line-up at cashier with an empty cart and then sends children to get items	Passive-Aggressive
• Insists on starting new diet right in the store — won't pay for book or food until results are seen	Schizotypal

Parking Lot

• Has items delivered directly to car	Schizoid
• Remains in car, scans surroundings with periscope before exiting	Paranoid
• Visits on *Customer Appreciation Day*	Avoidant
• Greets shoppers and introduces self as "Wal" from Wal-Mart	Narcissist

Newhart Was Never Like This:

Introduction
The ideal therapeutic group may well be composed of one of each of the DSM-IV-TR personality disorders. The following script shows typical, but hypothetical, interactions between the different character types.

Session Transcript
Narcissist: Well, I . . .

Obsessive: Nice try, but I have to call the session to order first.

Passive-Aggressive: This is a group session, not a board meeting, dufus.

Obsessive: What about circulating the minutes from last week's meeting? I have an indexed, collated and cross-referenced copy for everyone right here.

Schizotypal: You're such a yin force. Try some yang foods tonight. I'll make a list for you.

Therapist: We were all here. We're well acquainted with what went on.

Passive-Aggressive: That's quite an alliteration!

Obsessive: Well, I still have my agenda to deal with (looks at PDA). I've been reading a book called *Thinking About Feelings*.

Avoidant: Gee, that sounds really interesting. I wonder if it's available through my book club? I could use my bonus points to get us all a copy, that is, if it's OK with everybody.

Antisocial: (leaning towards Avoidant) I thought that, ahem, you know, you promised those bonus points to me in exchange for . . .

Therapist: It seems that we're forgetting the policy about contact outside the group. What's going on?

Antisocial: (glaring at Avoidant to ensure silence) My time and talent is worth money! Besides, she needed a date for the Correspondence Course Reunion.

Passive-Aggressive: Liberté, Egalité, mais pas de Fraternité, mes enfants.

Schizotypal: I'm sensing some bad karma right now. . .

Borderline: You Antisocial jerk! That's where you were! I waited up all night. I was so mad I got a headache and starting taking some pain killers, and then I overdosed on them. You made me do it!

Narcissist: He's not worth it. You should look for better men. (preens and then mutters audibly) No one ever overdosed because of me.

Therapist: I thought it was clear that group rules were meant . . .

Obsessive: To be obeyed and strictly enforced.

Antisocial: To be bent, and if need be, broken. There wouldn't be rules otherwise.

Schizoid: (freezes, then takes a renewed interest in shoelaces) Uh huh.

Schizotypal: Natural laws are too complex for human understanding.

Passive-Aggressive: (shrugs) *Whatever.*

Borderline: For others to deal with.

Narcissist: To be open to interpretation.

Histrionic: I don't know. I can't remember. Can someone remind me?
A guy, maybe?

Paranoid: To watch out for . . . or else.

Dependent: To get someone to explain them to you. I need help.

Avoidant: Wha. . wha. . whatever you say. The thought of all those new people just frightened me, and that Antisocial can be such a charmer.

Passive-Aggressive: So tell us what else happened between you two, or three, I guess it is now.

Histrionic: And don't spare any details!

Therapist: We're getting away from what Obsessive was saying.

Avoidant: I'm sorry, Obsessive. Did that make you feel . . . . . . upset?

Obsessive: No, actually, I never feel anything.

Schizotypal: Do you have a horoscope in that daytimer? What's a *non-sequitur* anyway? I never took Latin, but I hear there's voodoo in Latin America.

Narcissist: I don't think that's important right now. What makes our Obsessive and his book so special? I could bring a book next week. I've had a simply horrific week, and no time to air my concerns.

Schizotypal: I sense a split in the karma right now.

Paranoid: Is that good or bad? Both, or neither? Can it be harmful?

Borderline: Men are all the same, always me, Me, ME. Well, what about me? Guys seem so supportive at the beginning and then they just don't care. Women are the only truly nurturing beings. I hate all men.

Dependent: You're so right! I can't remember all the times I've been let down. You keep pouring yourself out and when you're in need, there's nobody there. I need some support right now to talk about this.

Schizotypal: There is a positive force descending upon us now.

Paranoid: But how long will it last? What happens next?

Borderline: I can't believe it . . . you really and truly understand me. Now that I think of it, you've always been there for me. Now that we have each other, maybe we don't need anyone else. (gets up and sits next to Dependent)

Histrionic: (gushes) I'm glad you're feeling better. I'm sooooo happy for you. I'll bring a card next week.

Obsessive: Shouldn't you at least do a feasibility study first?

Paranoid: Or at least a blood test or something?

Narcissist: Why not consider other options . . . I think you might find somebody wonderful very nearby.

Dependent: I wish I had the courage to just reach out like that.

Schizotypal: The celestial forces strongly oppose this union. The gravitational pull exerted by a Dependent Moon can only slightly alter the course of a Borderline Comet.

Passive-Aggressive: We all know it won't work. What's your opinion, Schizoid?

Schizoid: If everyone here pairs up . . . . I can be alone again.

Therapist: Our agreement is to talk about feelings, not act on them!

Antisocial: Really honey, not so fast — just like you heard here. I was planning to surprise you. The books were going to be a gift — you know how you've always wanted to study Social Psychology. It's just that, um, um, what's her name here, really gets going once you give her a chance. I was on the way to the hospital when I met a few old "business partners" and got side-tracked.

Avoidant: Well, it's back to fantasizing about online dating for me.

Therapist: We've got just a short time left. Maybe it's time to check in with Schizoid. What would you like to share with us today?

Schizoid: Uh . . . . nothing.

Narcissist: What do I have to do to get some air time here? Bring a book? Overdose? Say nothing and play with my shoelaces?

Paranoid: You've been dominating this group and my life for too long now, Narcissist. Watch out!

Obsessive: Maybe we could make a schedule for next session. I'll bring my stopwatch, make a schedule, and call everyone prior to the session so we can make it the best discussion ever.

Dependent: We could extend the time of the session — an eight-hour session would only leave sixteen in the day, and then there's my other groups. . .

Antisocial: Can we divide into little groups and change partners each week?

Borderline: Sounds like you do that anyway.

Passive-Aggressive: Small things amuse small minds . . .

Histrionic: While the smaller ones take note! I read that in *Cosmo.* You sure do learn a lot in those quizzes. Maybe we can all do one. I'll bring in some old issues next week.

Narcissist: Those quizzes are far too simple for this vapid sophisticate.

Obsessive: Sometimes I think you're just so neurotic.

Passive-Aggressive: He sure is.

Narcissist: Well if I am, so are you.

Therapist: Hold that thought, and we'll start there next week.

Paranopoly

GO TO JAIL — NEVER GET OUT

TAX TIME LOSE EVERY-THING

FREE PARKING — TOWING — NOT!

WATCH OUT!

TAKE A CHANCE **?**

MEET A LAWYER NAMED SUE!!

IS SOMEONE CHEATING?

PUBLIC UTILITIES DISCONNECTS YOUR WATER AND ELECTRICITY

GO AWAY!

GET TIED TO THE B.O.

TRACK

LOSE A TURN, NEXT TIME IT'S YOUR LIFE!

Fill-in-the-Blank Romance:
Anatomy of a Romance Novel

Act I

An unspoiled <u>histrionic</u> lives a marginal existence under the tyranny of her husband. However, she gave her word on the altar and remains deeply committed to this <u>schizoid</u> lout even though he is just a shell of the man she married. His frequent business trips don't arouse her suspicions until she is tipped off by his <u>paranoid</u> secretary that he is having an affair (with the same woman who broke up her own marriage). She seeks the comfort of her hapless <u>obsessive</u> boss who cannot contain himself and confesses his undying love for her.

Act II

Reeling from the betrayal of this trusted friendship, she enters a trance-like state and wastes away in her elegant apartment. In the nick of time, her trusty but highly <u>dependent</u> confidante offers her some banal advice which depresses her even more. Summoning her last ounce of strength, she sets out on a journey of recovery. Her life takes an intriguing twist when she takes the advice of a <u>schizotypal</u> fortune-teller and leaves for a distant, enchanting land.

Act III

The heat and lush, undulating landscape cause her to let down her guard and fall prey to the affections of a dashing, wealthy <u>narcissist</u>. Unbeknownst to her, libidinal strivings are simultaneously aroused in this man's nefarious, but strikingly handsome, <u>antisocial</u> brother. While being royally courted by these two, she catches a glimpse of a kindred spirit, the mysterious <u>avoidant</u> who works as a stable-hand.

Act IV

A long-seated rivalry between the two brothers reaches a fever pitch and they agree their dignity can only be settled by a duel. As high noon approaches, the <u>borderline</u> ex-lover of one of the brothers returns and quells his ire. Besides, the <u>passive-aggressive</u> matriarch of the family was fed up with her ill-tempered sons and loaded blanks in their duelling pistols.

Epilogue

As our heroine takes up with her man of mystique, clouds in the shape of wedding bells start to form on the horizon.

Fill-in-the-Blank Suspense:
Anatomy of a Bond Adventure

Act I
Bond, a government contracted <u>antisocial</u>, is summoned from some exotic locale where he is risking his life recreationally, instead of in the line of duty. His sadistic, <u>schizoid</u> boss, who has never even set foot outside the building to serve England, briefs him on an impossibly dangerous mission.

Bond picks up a great new gadget from the <u>schizotypal</u> in the research department. Though it seems cumbersome and the instructions tedious, it inevitably saves his life — only after he tries it out on a lowly <u>obsessive-compulsive</u> sap from elsewhere in the department.

Act II
Bond quickly dumps his <u>dependent</u> girlfriend, who actually portrayed the <u>histrionic</u> in the last adventure. His itinerary is abruptly changed when his boss's <u>passive-aggressive</u> secretary uses his plane tickets for her own vacation.

Act III
After arriving first class at an even more interesting destination than originally planned, he is enamored by the charms of the <u>borderline</u> sent by his nemesis. Although she plans to kill him, Bond's superficial charm persuades her to switch allegiances. In doing so, she pays with her life but not before revealing the identity of a gorgeous <u>avoidant</u> who is the right-hand assistant to the bad guy.

Act IV
Bond enlists the help of the local <u>paranoid</u> FBI/CIA/IRA/IBM/IRS agent with a soft spot for assisting the British. Though Bond prefers to work alone, the assistance he is invariably forced to accept enables him to defeat the evil empire built by the megalomaniac <u>narcissist</u>, and return the world to safety.

Epilogue
Bond takes full advantage of the post-traumatic effects of the recent mayhem on the heroine. On principle, he avoids returning to work for at least a fortnight while still collecting his full salary.

Aggressive

We met in the Uomo Menswear store; he had to steal a tie for his probation hearing. Blunt and direct, he was a man of few words, most of them having four letters.

Slick

He said I could call him Ted, Billy Ray, or Freddy — he had i.d. for each name. The sex was fast, furious and always in a public place. He missed his other girlfriend, and got her to join us after threatening to turn in her dealer.

Predatory

He wanted to commemorate the occasion with matching tattoos — black scorpions. It complemented the ones he already had — **NFA** on his left arm and **NRA** on the right. He promised the artist payment next week, but ended up ripping him off anyway.

Dangerous

We skipped his AA meeting; it only drove him to drink, and drive. So we did, racing another stolen car into the sunset. He handled it all like a pro — and said so.

Truly an **8-Ball** man.

The cologne for real men.

Sociopathy 101

Erik Erikson developed the now familiar stages of his *Life Cycle Theory*. In one of his first applications, he compared the anomalous development of the Singleton twins, one of whom called in a bomb threat the very night his brother was to receive the Nobel Peace Prize.

	Normal (Nobel Prize)	**Antisocial (No Prize)**
Stage 1	Trust vs. Mistrust	Lust vs. Misogyny
Stage 2	Autonomy vs. Shame & Doubt	Auto Theft vs. Doubtful Shame
Stage 3	Initiative vs. Guilt	Insanity Defense vs. Guilty Plea
Stage 4	Industry vs. Inferiority	Repeat Offender vs. Reform School
Stage 5	Identity vs. Identity Confusion	Narcissism vs. Phony Sincerity
Stage 6	Intimacy vs. Isolation	Gang Allegiance vs. Solitary Confinement
Stage 7	Generativity vs. Stagnation	Crime Spree vs. Collecting Social Assistance
Stage 8	Integrity vs. Despair	Most Wanted List vs. Two-Bit Reputation

Fill-in-the-blank Personalities:
Fatal Personalities Instinctively Attract

Act I
Seemingly out of nowhere, a talented, attractive and highly available borderline drops into the plot. A glimpse of her tortured past is given, but through a series of clever and evasive maneuvers in script writing, the details are concealed. She quickly gets the attention of a roving narcissist, and lavishes on him the attention that his dependent wife and schizoid child are not supplying in sufficient quantities for his hypertrophied ego.

Act II
Idealization runs rampant. They live. They love. They frolic. They Cluster B all over each other. They do things even a paranoid couldn't imagine, or a schizotypal wouldn't even foretell.

Act III
Eventually things get a little rough. He needs to get back to reality, she just needs more of him. He levels with his obsessive-compulsive friend, who draws up a twelve-step plan for her emotional independence, but it is of to no avail. Erratic job performance eventually comes to the attention of his avoidant boss, who after empathically hearing all the details, is forced to hand out a suspension.

Act IV — Option 1
Admitting his stupidity to his wife causes a re-emergence of her histrionic side, and the very qualities that drew them together in the first place They pool their antisocial qualities and devise a plan to rid themselves of his lover.

Act IV — Option 2
Events escalate to a histrionic pitch. He realizes life without his borderline lover would be dull, if she allowed him to have any. Together, they make a pact not to exploit each other's antisocial qualities, and live happily ever after, or at least until the next crisis.

InnerSpace

The interpersonal frontier . . . this is the saga of
the voyager Narcissus, on a five year journey to
seek a way out of the. . .

Egocentric Universe

Episode 1
Narcissus has a rendezvous with Comet Kohutek, encountering an
empathic betazoid species who mirror the prime directive.

Episode 2
Full battle
stations as
N a r c i s s u s
grapples with
Darth Kernberg,
and must make
use of the ship's
d e f e n s i v e
capabilities to
avoid a photon
interpretation.

First Date Checklist

❑5 packages of breath mints
❑Flowers
❑Bone for dog
❑Odor eaters (new)
❑Chocolates (good ones)
❑Cab fare home (plus tip)
❑Catnip for cat

❑Engagement ring
❑Triple-checked address
❑Food critic's review of restaurant
❑Conversation piece
❑Two watches to avoid being late
❑Picture of someone's baby
❑Book of 1000 compliments

Dependent's Apartment
(from first date with Avoidant Personality)

Rules of Order for the Malignant Obsessive-Compulsive Personality

- Being a Type A personality isn't good enough; strive for an A+.

- If in doubt, think, Think, THINK it out.

- The inkblot test has no time limit. After giving your response, clean up some of the mess.

- The more you do, and the faster you do it, the longer you live.

- If it's worth doing, it's worth over-doing.

- The best reward for hard work is more work.

- Encourage others to do it by the book, **your** book.

- Perfection is the lowest acceptable standard.

- You can get all the rest you need when you're dead.

- The words **compromise, choice** and **no** are not in your vocabulary.

- If you can't change the rules, change the game.

- There are others like you in every organization; seek them out!

- Burn the candle at both ends, then in the middle!

Lady Macbeth Knows Dirt!

Having to worry about cleaning everything
from delusional blood stains to Arabian
perfume, Lady M certainly had her hands full!
We obtained her famous *Dunsinane Castle*
formula and are now pleased to bring
you our new household cleaner,
Out Damned Spot! in honor of her ladyship.

Now available in liquid and capulet form.

The Fractionated Personality Disorder
by Morton Rapp, M.D.

The Multiple Personality Disorder (MPD), a malady in which "the essential feature . . . is the existence within the person of two or more distinct personalities or personality states,"[1] has gained much popularity in usage among members of the clinical community. This relatively new diagnostic entity has only been in vogue during the second half of this century. It remained rare until the 1950's, when scientific advances in the area were bolstered by two critical discoveries: (1) there's a sucker born every minute, and (2) books describing MPD were ultimately highly lucrative for the authors. Controversy has always surrounded MPD as a diagnosis. Its supporters claim that many patients who were subjected to severe child abuse early in their lives tend to evidence MPD later on, and further, that those who would challenge the validity of this may themselves suffer from MPD. The author feels that this diagnosis has heuristic value and presents here a related and ancillary disorder — the **Fractionated Personality Disorder (FPD)**.

Rationale:
In mathematics, every number has a reciprocal; for example, the reciprocal of 2 is 1/2. It follows logically that if individuals exist who have more than one personality, then there must be others with only a fraction of a personality in order that the fundamental equilibrium of the universe be maintained.

Empirical Base:
No studies have been performed to test the hypothesis of FPD. It was felt that the intrusion of coarse methods such as standardized interviews, or the intervention of psychiatric epidemiologists, would cheapen the area of study — and ruin the author's chances of success in launching his forthcoming book(s) on this diagnostic entity.

Etiology:
The specter of child abuse underlies much of the FPD, as illustrated in the following case:

M.R., a 16-year-old teenager of Yuppie background, had been enjoying a successful career as a malingerer until his 16th birthday. On that date, his father refused to buy him a Jaguar Sovereign, stating that the family's second car, a 5.0 liter Mustang, would have to do. The patient had a history of abuse at the hands of his father, namely being forced to study and refrain from using LSD. M.R., upon hearing the Jaguar was a no go, immediately stopped speaking and became a "1/3" personality, characterized by sleeping 14 hours per day and attending school one day out of three.

Clinical Features:

Despite a lack of lack of systematic study, workers in the field of FPD have identified a number of characteristic epidemiological features:

1. It afflicts all sexes.
2. It is more common in right-handed people.
3. In South-East Asia, it is more common in Asians, whereas in Europe, it is more common in whites.
4. Its highest incidence is between ages two to ninety-four.
5. It is surprisingly common among people who are in need of a clinical diagnosis to excuse some otherwise maladaptive behavior.
6. It has a high incidence among certain occupational groups (e.g. hospital administrators). However, it is conspicuously absent in lawyers, suggesting that these professionals may have no personality whatsoever.

Quantitative Ecology:

The diagnosis of FPD lends itself to easy quantification. For example:

$$p(FPD) = N + B^{(L/D)}$$

- p(FPD) is the probability of a clinical case suffering from FPD
- N is the number of current believers in the diagnostic entity
- B is the number of financially successful books on the topic
- L is the lurid nature of the FPD patient's history, in luridity units
- D is the number of detractors of the diagnostic entity (IQ > 90)

One fruitful avenue for investigation might be determining the smallest fraction of a personality to be found in an individual (e.g. from a clinician's perspective, a one-eighth personality would be four times more interesting than a one-half personality). As yet, there is no evidence to support the existence of an Exponential Personality (where the personality would be represented mathematically by two to the nth degree), or even a square root personality.

The author has described the presence of a diagnostic entity that supplements the Multiple Personality Disorder — the Fractionated Personality Disorder. The manuscripts for six books have already been completed and copyrighted by the author.

[1] American Psychiatric Association, 1987, Diagnostic and Statistical Manual of Mental Disorders, Third Edition Revised, Washington, DC

Index

— A —
Acting Up 59
Adaptation 4, 7
Affect 98
Agreeableness 87
Anancastic/Anankastic Personality
 Disorder 13
Antisocial Personality Disorder 9, 11,
 13, 47, 57, 92, 145, 174
Anxiety Disorders 98
Anxious Personality Disorder 13
Asthenic Personality Disorder 163
Attachment Theory   26, 33
Avoidant Personality Disorder
 9, 13, 14, 47, 57, 92, 101, 145, 177

— B —
Behavior 98
Bile, Various Types 27
Biopsychosocial Model   80
Biopsychosocial Management Plan
 81 - 85
Borderline Personality Disorder 9,
 13, 14, 47, 57, 92, 95, 145, 175
Bowlby, John   28, 30

— C —
Cerebral Personality Disorder 161
Character   86, 87, 93, 94, 95
 Cooperativeness 93, 94, 94
 Self-Directedness   93, 94, 95
 Self-Transcendence 93, 94, 95
Characteristic Adaptations 149
Chemical Imbalances 109
Circumplex 46
Clarification   45
Clusters, Personality Disorder 9, 15
 16, 98, 106, 145
Cognition 98
Cognitive Distortions
 Arbitrary Inference 42
 Assuming Temporal Causality 42
 Catastrophizing   42
 Dichotomous Thinking   42
 Excessive Responsibility 42
 Magnification/Minimization 42
 Overgeneralization 42

 Personalization   42
 Selective Abstraction   42
 Self-Reference 42
Cognitive Shift   41
Cognitive Therapy   40, 95
 Automatic Assumptions 41
 Negative Thoughts   41
Cognitive Triad of Depression 40
Collaborative Empiricism   41
Conduct Disorder   11
Confrontation 45
Conscientiousness   87
Conscious   52
Content, of Psychotherapy   37
Countertransference   14
Creative Effort   34
Cultural Examples   21, 22
Culture and Personality   20
Cyclothymic Personality Disorder
 164

— D —
Defense Mechanisms — see Ego
 Defense Mechanisms
Delusional Disorder   98
Dependent Personality Disorder 9,
 13, 14, 22, 47, 57, 92, 145, 178
Depression 40, 98
Depressive Personality Disorder 11
Dialectical Behavior Therapy   3
Diagnostic and Statistical Manual of
 Mental Disorders   3, 5 , 8, 9, 10,
  11, 12, 13, 140, 141, 159
Diagnostic Interviews 138
 Dependent Personality
  Questionnaire 138
 Diagnostic Interview for
  Narcissism 138
 Psychopathy Checklist - Revised
  138
 Schedule for Schizotypal
  Personalities 138
Dimensional Model   96, 100
Dissocial/Dyssocial Personality
 Disorder 13
Dissociative Disorders   156, 161

Dissociative Identity Disorder 154 - 157
Disturbances in Interpersonal Relationships 33
Dopamine 102, 106
Dreams, Interpretation of 52

— E —
Ego 53
Ego Defense Mechanisms 11, 49, 54, 55, 58 - 76
  Acting Out 55, 56, 57, 59, 95
  Anticipation 55, 56, 74
  Classification of 55
  Controlling 55, 56, 57, 60
  Denial 55, 56, 57, 60
  Displacement 55, 56, 57, 61
  Dissociation 55, 56, 57, 61
  Distortion 55, 56, 57, 62
  Humor 55, 56, 75
  Idealization/Devaluation 55, 56, 57, 62
  Identification 55, 56, 57, 64
  Inhibition 55, 56, 57, 64
  Intellectualization 55, 56, 57 65
  Introjection 55, 56, 57, 65
  Isolation of Affect 55, 56, 57, 66
  Mnemonic 56
  Passive -Aggression 55, 56, 57, 66
  Projection 55, 56, 57, 67
  Projective Identification 55, 56, 57, 67 - 69
  Rationalization 55, 56, 57, 70
  Reaction Formation 55, 56, 57 70
  Regression 55, 56, 57, 71
  Schizoid Fantasy 55, 56, 57, 71
  Sexualization 55, 56, 57, 72
  Somatization 55, 56, 57, 72
  Splitting 55, 56, 57, 73
  Sublimation 55, 56, 75
  Undoing 55, 56, 57, 73
Egosyntonic 5, 88
Emotionally Unstable Personality Disorder 13
Erikson, Erik 28, 29, 142, 143
Explosive Personality Disorder 93, 165
Extraversion 87

Evil Eye 22

— F —
Fight Response 4, 33
Five Factor Model(s) 87, 148
Flight Response 4, 33
Formulation 80
Freud, Sigmund 28, 32, 87
Freudian Slips 37

— G —
General Diagnostic Criteria for a Personality Disorder 10
General Medical Conditions 11
Global Assessment of Functioning Score 11
Group Therapy 43
  Therapeutic Factors in 44
Guided Discovery 41

— H —
Harm Avoidance 88, 89, 90, 91, 92
Histrionic Personality Disorder 9, 13, 14, 47, 57, 92, 173

— I —
Id 53
Imaginary Companions 156
Impulse-Control Disorders 98, 99
Inadequate Personality Disorder 162
Integrated Classification System 15
International Classification of Diseases, 10th Edition 13
Interpersonal Therapy 45, 46, 47
  Prototypic Wishes 47
Interpretation(s) 45
  Peer 45
Introversion 87

— L —
Life Cycle Stages 28

— M —
Mahler, Margaret 28, 31
Major Clinical Disorders 11
Mania/Manic Episode 98
Masochism
Masochistic Personality 158 - 159
Medication, Types
  Antidepressants 102, 106, 107
  Antipsychotics 102, 106

Anxiolytics 102, 107
Mood Stabilizers 102, 106, 107
Sedative-Hypnotics 102
Stimulants 102
Medication, Selection 104, 105
Medication, Separate Providers
111 - 112
Medication, Special Considerations
109, 110, 111, 112
Memory
Declerative 86
Procedural 86
Mental Retardation 11
Mental Status Examination 99, 138
Millon Clinical Multiaxial Inventory
88, 127
Misbehaving 59
Mood Disorders (general) 98, 99,
156, 161
Multiaxial Format/System 11, 12, 141,
142
Multiple Personality Disorder
154 - 157

— N —
Narcissistic Personality Disorder 9,
13, 14, 47, 57, 92, 145, 176
Negativistic Personality Disorder 9
Neuroticism 87
Norepinephrine 102, 106
Novelty Seeking 88, 89, 90, 91, 92

— O —
Object Relations Theory 26, 33, 34,
35, 36
Objective Tests 116, 121 - 137
Borderline Personality
Organization Scale 121
Coolidge Assessment Battery 122
Diagnostic Interview for
Borderlines, Revised 123
Dimensional Assessment of
Personality Pathology - Basic
Questionnaire 124
Eysenck Personality
Questionnaire - Revised 125
International Personality Disorder
Examination 126
Millon Clinical Multiaxial
Inventory - Third Edition 88, 127

Minnesota Multiphasic Personality
Inventory 128
NEO Five-Factor Inventory 129
NEO Personality Inventory -
Revised 129
Omni-IV Personality Disorder
Inventory 130
Personality Assessment Inventory
130
Personality Assessment Schedule
131
Personality Diagnostic
Questionnaire 131
Personality Disorder Interview
132
Schedule for Nonadaptive and
Adaptive Personality 133
Standardized Assessment of
Personality 134
Structured Clinical Interview for
DSM-IV Axis II Personality
Disorders 135
Structured Interview for DSM-IV
Personality Disorders 135
Structured Interview for the
Five-Factor Model of
Personality 136
Wisconsin Personality Disorders
Inventory 137
Obsessive-Compulsive Disorder 161
Obsessive-Compulsive Personality
Disorder 9, 13, 14, 22, 47, 57, 92,
145, 179
Oedipal Complex/Conflict/Stage
36, 53, 58
Organic Personality 160 - 161

— P —
Paranoid Personality Disorder 9, 11,
13, 14, 47, 57, 93, 101, 145, 171
Parapraxes 37
Passive-Aggressive Personality
Disorder 9, 11, 93, 145
Perception 98
Personality 4, 86
Personality Change Due to a General
Medical Condition 17, 160 - 161
Personality Disorder(s) 5, 140, 145
Severity Specifiers 12
Personality Disorder Not Otherwise
Specified 9, 11

Personality Traits 11
Phobias, General 161
Phobia, Social 101
Piaget, Jean 4
Pleasurable Interpersonal
  Relationships 33
Posttraumatic Stress Disorder 156,
  161
Preconscious 52
Primary Process 52
Projection 37
Projective Tests 116, 117 - 120
  Forer Structured Sentence
    Completion Test 117
  Holtzman Inkblot Test 118
  Rorschach Ink Blots 119
  Rotter Incomplete Sentences
    Blank 119
  Thematic Apperception Test 120
Process of Psychotherapy 37
Psyche 78
Psychic Determinism 37
Psychodynamic Therapy 95
Psychological Testing 116
Psychometric Testing 116
Psychosocial and Environmental
  Problems 11
Psychotherapy 26, 146, 149
Psychotic Disorders 98, 101, 156, 161
Psychosomatic 78, 79
Psychosomatic Medicine 79
Psychoticism 87, 125

— R —
Repression 54, 58, 56, 57, 58
  Primary 58
  Secondary 58
Resistance 39, 52
Reward Dependence 88, 89, 90, 91,
  92

— S —
Sadism 159
Sadistic Personality 159
Schema 41
Schizoid Personality Disorder 9, 11,
  13, 14, 47, 57, 92, 93, 145, 170
Schizophrenia — see Psychotic
  Disorders
Schizotypal Disorder 13

Schizotypal Personality Disorder 9, 11,
  14, 47, 57, 92, 93, 145, 172
Secondary Process 52
Self Disorders 15
Self-Defeating Personality 158 - 159
Serotonin 102
Seven-Factor Model 93
Signal Axiety 54
Social Evolutionary Strategies 7
Social Phobia 101
Social Skills Training 95
Socratic Questioning 41
Soma 78
Somatoform Disorders 161
Spectrum Disorders 15
Structural Analysis of Social
  Behavior 46
Structural Theory 53
Substance Use Disorders 156
Superego 53
Suppression 55, 56, 57, 58
Symptom Versatility in Personality
  Disorders 14

— T —
Temperament 86, 87, 93, 94, 95, 96,
  148
  Activity Level 87
  Adaptability 87
  Approach/Withdrawal 87
  Attention Span/Persistence 87
  Distractibility 87
  Intensity of Reaction 87
  Persistence 93
  Quality of Mood 87
  Rhythmicity 87
  Threshold of Responsiveness
    87
  Treatment of 96
Temperament and Character
  Inventory 94
Topographic Theory 52
Trait Disorders 15
Transference 37
Transitional Object(s) 110

— U —
Unconscious 37, 52, 59

— W —
World Health Organization 13

The Author

Dave Robinson is a psychiatrist practicing in London, Ontario, Canada. His particular interests are general adult inpatient psychiatry, in addition to undergraduate and postgraduate education. A graduate of the University of Toronto Medical School, he completed a Residency in Family Practice before entering Psychiatry. He is a faculty member and former Residency Training Director in the Department of Psychiatry at the University of Western Ontario in London, Canada.

The Artist

Brian Chapman is a resident of Manitoulin Island, Ontario, Canada. He was born in Sussex, England and moved to Canada in 1957. His first commercial work took place during W.W. II when he traded drawings for cigarettes while serving in the British Navy. Now retired, Brian was formerly a Creative Director at Mediacom. He continues to freelance and is versatile in a wide range of media. He is a master of the caricature, and his talents are constantly in demand. He is married to Brenda, a retired principal, fellow artist, and world traveler. Brian is an avid trumpet player and performs regularly with a variety of bands.

Rapid Psychler Press produces textbooks and resource materials that further the use of humor in psychiatric education. In addition to textbooks, Rapid Psychler specializes in producing 35mm slides, overhead transparencies, and digital graphics for presentations.

Rapid
Psychler®
Press